AFFIRMING
LOVE

AFFIRMING LOVE

REFLECTIONS INTO THE
HEART OF GOD

CHRISTINE LEONARD

My thanks to Sue Doggett,
who not only edited this book but
encouraged and inspired.
But for her, it wouldn't
have been written.

Text copyright © Christine Leonard 1999

The author asserts the moral right
to be identified as the author of this work

Published by
The Bible Reading Fellowship
Peter's Way, Sandy Lane West
Oxford OX4 5HG
ISBN 1 84101 052 9

First published 1999
10 9 8 7 6 5 4 3 2 1 0

A catalogue record for this book
is available from the British Library

Printed and bound in Great Britain by
Caledonian Book Manufacturing International, Glasgow

CONTENTS

A Better Resurrection

My life is like a broken bowl,
A broken bowl that cannot hold
One drop of water for my soul
Or cordial in the searching cold;
Cast in the fire the perished thing,
Melt and remould it, till it be
A royal cup for him my King:
O Jesus, drink of me.

Christina Rossetti (1830–94)

INTRODUCTION

God is… big. Enormous. More vast than I could ever think or imagine—and God is love (1 John 4:8). The scope and depth of his love, the creative ways in which it reaches people, go way beyond my imagination.

God's love is important, the most important thing ever. Goethe (1749–1832) said, 'We are shaped and fashioned by what we love.' Jesus told us to love others only because he first loved us (John 13:34). If Christianity is about our relationship with God, the quality of the flow of love between us is fundamental, influencing everything else in our lives. According to the shorter catechism the chief end of humankind is 'to glorify God and enjoy him forever'. If I don't know that God loves me, then it's very hard to enjoy him or to love others.

So what is love? It can't be weighed and measured scientifically. How do I know that my husband loves me? Twenty years ago he made certain promises. I can produce the certificate to prove it, but I don't think we'd have a very real or loving marriage on that basis alone. I know he loves me because he shows me his love in all kinds of ways, through words, practical help, prayer and support, through thoughtfulness, caring for or (occasionally) rebuking me, through laughter, touch, passion, forgiveness, encouragement and sacrifice, through wanting to spend time with me—sharing plans, tasks, dreams, worries, discoveries, disappointments and successes, through teaching me things, or buying me something special, through being patient and faithful. He shows his love in so many ways, and it's the same with God; God shows his love for us in all these ways and more.

What words can describe God's love and even begin to show its immensity, or the way it's fresh and new every morning? The Bible uses imagery or picture language, as do religious poetry and hymns (and love songs and poems, when describing human love). Images of God's love occur throughout scripture—the good shepherd, the father who cannot disown his wandering son, the patient gardener. This picture language spoke to people hundreds of years before Christ—and it speaks to us today. Biblical images are developed in later writing, but sometimes new ones emerge too. For example 'oceans' of God's love appear in many hymns, songs and poems, old and new, but never in the Bible! (To find out why, read the chapter called 'Oceans of love', page 141.) In this book I've developed images based mainly on scripture but have also used some from daily life, to show how God reveals his love to 'ordinary' Christians today.

Some people have a definite blockage to knowing, really knowing, that God loves them and it was for them that I had a special concern in writing.

'I know in my head that God loves me, but I've never been able to *feel* that he does!' The speaker sat on my sofa, her eyes miserable, staring past me.

She explained how she'd been following Jesus for three years. At first it had been so exciting, transforming her life, but now a grey plateau stretched in front of her. She remained grateful that Jesus had died for her, but her relationship with him had gone cold. She tried to do all the things Christians were supposed to do, like pray and love people and steer away from anything occult. But people had let her down and somehow she couldn't trust that God wouldn't walk out on her, too. She couldn't bring herself to believe that he really did love and value her.

I showed her some verses in the Bible.

'I never knew God rejoices over us with singing!' she said. 'That's amazing! Where did you say that verse was? In Zephan—who?'

She got so excited that I wished I could give her a book full of verses about God's love. I felt that she needed to bask in the truth of his love, to read maybe one verse a day. That way it might sink in, like penetrating oil, seeping into every part of her life, breaking down the barriers which had built up around jagged hurts, blocking love's flow. I'd never been able to find what I wanted—a book which would take both well-known and less familiar Bible passages and somehow catch the reader by surprise, giving a glimpse into the beating heart of Jesus' love for every individual.

Joyce Grenfell told the story of a small boy who was asked, 'What do you think God is?' He replied, 'God isn't a think, he's a feel!' I've met so many adults who find it hard to feel that God loves them. Some have been Christians for decades, others hover at the edges of faith. But is it important to feel his love? Blaise Pascal (1623–62), that great mathematician and philosopher, said, 'It is the heart that experiences God and not the reason.' While Christian truth is entirely reasonable and based on historical fact, it's never abstract. Its truth comes through a relationship with the person, Jesus—the only one who ever claimed to *be* the truth, the truth that will set us free.

So how does God, how does Jesus, show his love to us today? While researching this book, as well as trawling through the Bible and other literature, I accosted any Christian I met with the question, 'How do you feel God's love for you?' People started running away when they saw me coming, until I reassured them that this was no trick question with right or wrong answers. Once they'd overcome their reticence over such 'personal' matters, once they'd muttered shyly that they 'weren't quite sure really', they told me things which bowled me over and sparked my imagination. I've incorporated many of those insights on these pages and would like to take this opportunity to thank the people, most of whom chose to remain anonymous.

I didn't talk to haloed saints with hours to spend in mystical devotions, nor to professional clergy or 'big names'. Ordinary Christians are wonderful. They don't float around all gooey-eyed and lovey-dovey. Like me, they struggle with life's problems. Yet I found that just about everyone I approached had stories to tell of ways in which God had affirmed his special love for them—especially at dark times when they needed him most.

It's all too easy to dismiss true stories, because the other person's circumstances seem irrelevant to one's own life. I know God shows his love through 'God-incidences' of practical care or sending the right person at the crucial moment, but on this occasion I wasn't looking for that kind of tale. Instead, people told me about images which God had tailor-made to convince them of his special love, often in a time of great need. For example, one woman who especially loved flowers explained how, when she was praying alone in a chapel at a very painful time in her life, she 'saw' a beautiful golden lily slowly opening its petals. She'd always enjoyed looking into the heart of flowers, appreciating their intricate detail. As she looked into the heart of this lily it was glowing, glowing gold. She knew it symbolized Jesus' special love for her and she hung on to that image; she hangs on to it still. I know because her face glowed as she told me of it, even though she spoke through tears and the circumstances which had caused her problems still remain dire.

I'll never forget visiting a group of thirty or so elderly women who meet every Monday afternoon to enjoy a cup of tea, a few hymns and prayers and a short talk. Having been billed as their speaker one week, I decided to risk asking my question, 'How do you feel God's love?' I acknowledged I was setting them quite a challenge and asked them to think first how they felt the love of a person—a friend or husband. I suggested they might feel that love through a tone of voice, a look or a hug, 'But God is a Spirit without arms or audible voice,' I said, 'so how do you feel his love?'

They weren't used to anyone asking them questions in this way, but once they got the idea they all started talking at once. 'I'm afraid I disagree with you,' someone said. 'I *have* felt God's arms around my shoulders. I was just setting off to work on my bike. Things were bad. I was really down in the dumps. There was no one else within sight and I knew those arms around my shoulders were God's. It lifted me and made such a difference, I've never forgotten it!'

'I've felt his arms too, just like that,' said another.

'And I've heard God's voice,' said a third. 'It was a commanding voice. I was lying on my bed praying because I had only a few minutes left before I had to take an important decision. The hospital said I should have an X-ray, but my GP thought it expensive and unnecessary. I was all alone in my room and I heard God's commanding voice saying, "Go!"' The X-ray spotlighted cancer; she received treatment and is now clear.

I'm not sure how many of these women had told others about these instances, remembered so clearly, sometimes from years beforehand. But that day it was as though floodgates had opened. All were telling each other stories and none wanted to go home. I don't know who was more encouraged, them or me. I'd been reading an article about great Christian mystics but, I tell you, they had nothing on the women in that meeting!

I wanted to tell their stories, because it's faith-building to know that God keeps affirming his love to ordinary Christians in real, tangible ways—in life as well as through books and images. I'm fascinated too by how people experience his love in different ways at different stages of their lives. When a man in my church heard that I was writing this book he handed me a poem which he had written—and with that I'll end this introduction. I pray that both Eric's poem and the chapters which follow will help you experience more of God's affirming love in your own life.

The Voice on the Mountain

I'd climbed the mountain of life,
I was young and I was brave
In this mighty cutting wind, this knife—
Surely the Lord would speak in this wind.
But the Lord was not in the wind.

I grew older and stronger still,
I knew more of my mountain
Of its moods and of its will,
I knew only an earthquake could shake it.
But the Lord was not in the earthquake.

Surely then, in this fire, here surely
For now I had learned wisdom.
This terrible all-consuming fury,
Surely God will speak in the fire.
But the Lord was not in the fire.

I've grown old in serving my God,
Now I lean on my stick,
My wisdom I see as a small thing;
And I shelter here in this cleft in the rock,
And I do not expect God to speak to me, not me.

But I go out and stand on the mountain,
And he does speak to me sometimes,
Answers my doubting and questions,
At the end of the day, at night-time
Quietly, in a still, small voice.

Eric Leat

HOW TO USE THIS BOOK

I've devoted each short chapter to a different aspect of God's love.
Each starts with a kind of scene-setter, a story, a sketch—try not
to look at the Bible verse until you have read this. Sometimes Bible
passages become so familiar that they fail to impact us any more,
but I hope that some tiny part of the truth and feeling behind
God's love will surprise you through these scene-setters. Having
read the Bible verses which follow, you might find the prayers and
meditations helpful in sparking off your own devotions based
around that particular aspect of God's love in your life. Or you
may be inspired by the poems or prose, which develop the theme
further. Many of them were written by people who knew the real-
ity of God's love in times past. I hope that their reflections will add
another dimension, emphasizing that God has always made his
love known to humankind. You may also find that the various
passages around a given topic spark off ideas for creative ways to
portray the love of God in church services and so on.

Read slowly, one chapter at a time, rather than all in one sitting.
Because God's love is so huge we can't experience it all at once.
Breaking it down into different aspects splits the dazzle of its white
light into rainbow colours which we can more comfortably examine and enjoy. Turning over the page to a new chapter is like turning the prism. Each colour may help us to see part of his love in
fresh ways.

It's a concept found in the Bible. The Greek word 'poikilos'
means variegated, chequered, many coloured, diverse, manifold—
as in 1 Peter 4:10, 'Like good stewards of the *manifold* grace of

God, serve one another with whatever gift each of you has received', or Ephesians 3:10, 'that through the church the wisdom of God *in its rich variety* might now be made known'. Of course some 'colours' may appeal to one person more than others. For example, those whose early relationships with their own fathers proved difficult can struggle with experiencing the loving fatherhood of God. But it's my prayer for this book that everyone who reads it will bathe in a growing spectrum of the light of his love. I pray that you will experience his love, not for the brief moments it takes to read the words, but that you will allow yourself to soak and swim in the river of his love, to drink deep of it and then drink again. I believe this is how we can hope to become more like him and so better reflect the light of his love to all around us.

BEGINNINGS

Today was another scorcher. I'd seen them start work early; bless them, there's so much they want to do! They're excellent gardeners. I keep a fatherly eye on them, of course. I glimpsed them, early on, pruning branches off that bush which had grown right over the path; even then they were sweating in the heat. By midday all they could do was to sprawl in the shade, tweaking the odd weed which lay within reach but otherwise stirring from their contented doze only when she slipped off in search of cool, fresh water or he sauntered over to the old plum tree to pick some lunch. It was too hot to eat much!

Around five, as the shadows lengthened across the garden, they roused themselves and gave the thirstier plants a drink. They were soon splashing each other, like children, and their laughter drifted towards me. They'll want supper soon, but afterwards, as the light begins to fade from the sky and the lightest of breezes dips the air to a delicious coolness, we'll stroll around the garden as usual, the three of us together, telling each other about our day.

With all work done, this has become a favourite time for all of us. They may be newly-weds, but three is never a crowd. We share our thoughts and our jokes and our plans—such big plans. There's nothing we can't say because we understand one another so well. Yet we discover fresh things about each other all the time, just as the garden yields surprises at every turn and in every season—the intricate pattern on a cyclamen leaf, the silken smoothness of that silver and ochre bark, the way one plant complements another. And that intriguing smell, drifting on the breeze—does it come from some hidden blossom or from a herb crushed beneath our feet?

We walk together in the garden, in the cool of the evening, utterly relaxed, utterly contented. Call me foolish, but I take more delight in the young couple with each day that passes. What joy, as a father, to see some of your own qualities played out in your children in new and creative ways. What joy to see them so happy! 'Perfection,' Eve sighs, for all the world like a cat, purring sleepily in the warmth of its owner's lap. Adam stands there, tall and strong, ruffling her hair and smiling at me. I'm so proud of them and I want everyone to know it!

Then, after the silken night, they will wake to the fresh discoveries of another day, a day in which their good plans for their children's children and for the world will come a little nearer fruition. Yes, we have made the best of starts. Already life's as full as I intended it to be from the beginning and, as our love for each other grows ever deeper, it can only go on getting better.

So God created man in his own image, in the image of God he created him; male and female he created them. And God blessed them, and God said to them, 'Be fruitful and multiply, and fill the earth and subdue it...' And the Lord God planted a garden in Eden, in the east; and there he put the man whom he had formed... And they [the man and his wife] heard the sound of the Lord God walking in the garden in the cool of the day.

Genesis 1:27–28; 2:8; 3:8 (RSV)

Meditation

Adam and Eve weren't surprised to hear God walking in the garden in the cool of the evening. It's not clear whether the story means that he showed himself to them in the form of a human or simply through his almost tangible presence with them. It does suggest something unimaginably close though—man, woman and God talking and walking together with no barriers between them, able to be totally themselves, with no self-conscious embarrass-ment, no hidden motivation, no hurts to be avoided, no pride or insecurity to be defended.

It's not easy for us to even begin to understand with our minds what that must have been like, that closeness, that free delight in each other. Perhaps you could stop and talk to God now—ask him to show you a little about his love for people and his delight in them. Take time to be quiet and let him show you. You may find it helpful to think of yourself walking hand in hand through a garden with Jesus. You're not looking for things which are wrong; in this garden even the slugs and snails are wonderful! You might like to read the beginning of Genesis and ask him in what way people are made in the image of God. Or you might like simply to tell him about your day and to ask him what he enjoyed about it.

> *How like an angel came I down!*
> *How bright are all things here!*
> *When first among His works I did appear*
> *O how their glory did me crown!*
> *The world resembled His eternity,*
> *In which my soul did walk;*
> *And everything that I did see*
> *Did with me talk...*
>
> *A native health and innocence*
> *Within my bones did grow,*
> *And while my God did all His glories show*
> *I felt a vigour in my sense*
> *That was all spirit. I within did flow*
> *With seas of life like wine.*
> *I nothing in the world did know*
> *But 'twas divine.*

From 'Wonder',
by Thomas Traherne (1637–74)

I think of God
And how he trod
That garden long ago;
He walked, I reckon, to and fro
And then sat down
Upon the groun'
Or some low limb
What suited him
Such as you see
On many a tree,
And on thik very one
Where I at set o' sun
Do sit and talk wi' he…

He never pushed the garden door,
He left no footmark on the floor;
I never heard 'un stir nor tread,
And yet his hand do bless my head,
And when 'tis time for work to start
I takes him with me in my heart…

From 'Under a Wiltshire Apple Tree',
by Anna Bunston (late 19th century)

A FATHER'S LOVE

The desert's hot and dusty—a lonely place. It's good for exploring—exploring the hidden landscape of your own being, as well
as the exposed heights of the spiky rocks and the slippery down-
falls of the dunes. All this takes heroic effort. Alone there, you're
as remote from kindness as you are from the moon. You understand thirst—a thirst for water, oranges and sweet dates, a thirst to
bathe in clear, running water, but most of all a thirst for compan-
ionship, for laughter, for someone to share the beauty and appreciate the effort. However much you may achieve, in the end all
seems as choking dust. I longed, how I longed, for grapes in the
desert. I dreamed of the first fruit of the fig tree in its first season,
of warm life, of newness and growth.

And that's how I found him—my son—and it was like stum-
bling across a young fig tree amid vast tracts of barrenness. He was
skin-touch and laughter. Comforting and protecting him tasted
better than cool water to a man dying of thirst. When I caught him
up in my arms his vulnerability melted my heart. I ran and jumped
and hid with him; his playfulness was my delight. I relaxed with
him in my arms, his sleeping head next to my heart—my boy! He
and I would do such great things together!

I searched out the best food for him and watched him grow
strong. I held him by the arms, let him kick with his legs, bounc-
ing up and down, crowing with delight. I crawled and rolled with
him over the sand. I taught him to walk, to trot, to run. I showed
him how to throw and how to find food for himself in the desert. I
cleared the stones from his path, picked him up when he stumbled,

told him how well he was doing and held out my hands so that he could run to me again. I taught him so many things, telling him each day that I loved him—and he called me 'Daddy'. He would fling himself at me off rocks, never doubting that I would catch him. He asked endless questions, trusting that I would always answer wisely. I took him exploring by starlight, scrambling over high peaks and pushing through narrow gorges with him—and always he clamoured for more.

I kept him on a good path—the one which seems narrow at first but which leads to a wide place. Though I saw us remaining close always, my love for him had nothing to do with apron-strings. I was training him to grow strong, to decide for himself—training him for true freedom. I wanted him to work with me on great deeds, not as a servant but as a partner, because I truly valued his contribution. In doing that I risked all. He turned from me, my son. He turned against me. In truth I should wipe him from the face of the earth, wipe all remembrance of him from my heart, but I cannot. I cannot. Tell me, if you are able, how shall I live with this tearing grief which overcomes me now, strong though I am?

> *Like grapes in the wilderness,*
> *I found Israel.*
> *Like the first fruit on the fig tree,*
> *in its first season...*
> *When Israel was a child, I loved him,*
> *and out of Egypt I called my son...*
> *Yet it was I who taught*
> *Ephraim to walk,*
> *I took them up in my arms;*
> *but they did not know that I healed them.*
> *I led them with cords of human kindness,*
> *with bands of love.*
> *I was to them like those who lift infants to their cheeks.*
> *I bent down to them and fed them...*
> *My people are bent on turning away from me...*
> *How can I give you up, Ephraim?*
> *How can I hand you over, O Israel?...*

My heart recoils within me;
my compassion grows warm and tender.
I will not execute my fierce anger...

Hosea 9:10; 11:1–9

Meditation

God feels these things for us! Adrian Plass wrote the following poem in response to this passage from Hosea. The perspective shocks me into seeing Father God's love and dilemma in a new way.

Forgive us if we say
We want to take you in our arms
Sad Father, weeping God
Breathless with the storms
Of anger—of compassion
Fists clenched hard around your grief
Around the marks
The cost
The proof
How can you give us up?
How can you hand us over?
Of course you never can
Never could
Never will
Burdened with perfection and with passion
Lay your head down
Let us hold you for a while
We will try to be to you
What you have been to us so many times
Peace, Lord, be a child once again
Do you remember Mary's arms?
So warm
So different

Rest quietly and soon you will be strong enough
To be a lion thundering from way beyond the east
We will come trembling from the west
We promise you
Like birds
Like doves
Like children who have suddenly remembered
Who taught them how to laugh
But just for now
Forgive us if we say
We want to take you in our arms
Sad Father, weeping God.

He's the father with the breaking heart, who looks each day for the return of his prodigal son. Yet many people find it hard to experience the father love of God because their own fathers were (or are) remote, cruel, domineering or even abusive. The twisting of love is more terrible, more fundamental than the pollution of pure water. Yet both water and love at source are pure—and shunning them brings nothing but thirst and weakness. Jesus said it is the truth that sets us free, so maybe the cure involves us soaking in the well-spring purity of Father God's love, until the pollution dilutes and drains slowly, imperceptibly away.

I find it helpful sometimes to think of myself as a small child, climbing up on God the Father's knee. He doesn't demand that I've succeeded in something, but he loves being with me; he wants to hear about my day and he enjoys the cuddle as much as I do. At other times I see myself, again as a small child, running towards him through a field of buttercups. He sweeps me up breathless into his arms and spins me round until we're both dizzy and laughing.

Behold what manner of love the Father has bestowed on us,
that we should be called children of God!

1 John 3:1 (NKJ)

And because you are children, God has sent the Spirit of his Son into our hearts, crying, 'Abba! Father!' So you are no longer a slave but a child, and if a child then also an heir, through God.

Galatians 4:6–7

My blood so red
For thee was shed,
Come home again, come home again:
My own sweet heart, come home again!
You've gone astray
Out of your way,
Come home again, come home again!

'The Call', Anonymous (17th century)

LOVE AS DISCIPLINE

This piece was written by a friend of mine who was going through a tough time. The worst part was all the set-backs...

'I dreamed I was on a journey. I'd started alone, wearing bedroom slippers—nothing seems odd in a dream. I was carrying a skipping-rope, a treasure map and a canary in a cage! Soon the gentle rolling countryside became steeper and more hazardous. I began to feel the stones under my feet. Only then did I realize that my slippers weren't suitable. God was telling me to go back to base. He came too and helped me find some sturdy walking boots.

'I set off again and, after a while, came to a cliff. I looked at the skipping-rope. I'd carried it quite happily without thinking about it, but now that I needed something to help me climb, I knew this toy was all wrong—too short, not strong enough! I had no alternative but to return to base and find a proper climber's rope.

'Setting off from there once again, I found myself in an unfamiliar area and had no idea which path to choose. I needed a map, but the one I carried pointed to treasure on some desert island—useless, since it had nothing to do with this place. I had to go back for the right map.

'My next attempt took me quite a way on the journey, but then I came to a place where, despite the good map's help, I needed a guide. I looked for my dog, but (how stupid!) I was holding a canary in a cage—a pet, yes, but the wrong species altogether. I had to go back to base once again. It would take a long time!

'This was frustrating. I seemed to be going nowhere and accomplishing nothing. And then I realized that wasn't true. Sure, I went back to base for boots, but when I returned for the rope at least I was kitted out in the correct footwear. When I returned for the map I had the right boots and rope, and when I went for the dog I had the right boots, rope and map. At each stage I became stronger and better prepared for the journey.

'I've remembered this dream because it made me smile and also because it helped me to see things from a different perspective. I wanted to push ahead, but God knew me better; he knew that I needed strengthening one stage at a time—and he loved me so much that he didn't care how long it took. To him, I was more important than the journey.'

'My child, do not regard lightly the discipline of the Lord,
or lose heart when you are punished by him;
for the Lord disciplines those whom he loves,
and chastises every child whom he accepts.' ...
[Our parents] disciplined us for a short time as seemed best to them,
but he disciplines us for our good,
in order that we may share his holiness.
Now discipline always seems painful rather than pleasant at the time,
but later it yields the peaceful fruit of righteousness
to those who have been trained by it.
Therefore lift your drooping hands and strengthen your weak knees,
and make straight paths for your feet,
so that what is lame may not be put out of joint,
but rather be healed.

Hebrews 12:5–6, 10–13

Meditation

Father, I don't like discipline, I never have. The walls of my teenage bedroom must have heard some choice ravings. My parents were ruining my life. They hadn't only thwarted my will once again, they'd dented my pride. Nothing was ever so unfair. I had been totally in the right. Obviously they, and the whole world, hated me.

The shame of it was I felt powerless because, despite my assertions, deep down I knew how much my parents loved me, sheltered me, cared for me. I wasn't going to run away from that, so I felt trapped. I was going to have to accept the truth in what they were saying. A friend envied me. Her parents didn't care what she did, or what time she came in; they seemed to have lost all interest. Yes, love does trap me, Lord, but I'd rather have it any day than the cold, empty, selfish lawlessness sometimes known as 'freedom'.

As for you, Father, just when I get comfortable, you have this habit of disturbing me—prodding me to try something new and a bit difficult. When I feel I'm doing pretty well, that my life's attaining some significance and my opinions are near infallible, you deflate me, ever so gently. When I feel I'm hearing your voice clearly and set off at a gallop in one direction, I bump into a wall and fall flat on my face. Then you pick me up, dust me down, give me a hug and tell me how special I am to you.

'No,' you say, smiling, 'you haven't ruined my eternal plans for the entire galaxy, you've simply taken another tumble—and tumbles are the only way any of my children learn to walk.'

> *Batter my heart, three-person'd God; for, you*
> *As yet but knock, breathe, shine, and seek to mend;*
> *That I may rise, and stand, o'erthrow me, and bend*
> *Your force, to break, blow, burn and make me new...*
> *Take me to you, imprison me, for I*
> *Except you enthral me, never shall be free,*
> *Nor ever chaste, except you ravish me.*

From 'Holy Sonnet XIV'
by John Donne (1572–1631)

I asked God to take away my pride, and God said No.
He said it was not for him to take away, but for me to give up.
I asked God to make my handicapped child whole and God said No.
He said her spirit is whole, her body is only temporary.
I asked God to grant me patience, and God said No.
He said that patience is a by-product of tribulation,
it isn't granted, it's earned.
I asked God to give me happiness, and God said No.
He said he gives blessings—happiness is up to me.
I asked God to spare me pain, and God said No.
He said suffering draws you apart from worldly cares
and brings you closer to me.
I asked God to make my spirit grow, and God said No.
He said I must grow on my own, but he will prune me
to make me fruitful.
I asked God to help me love others as much as he loves me,
And God said: 'Ah, finally you have the idea.'

'And God Said No', by Olive Dean

A MOTHER'S LOVE

How did he begin? With a longing—a love, a passion and yet more longing. A decision, brief moments of sublime joy, then nothing to show but this sick exhaustion. Devastated, overwhelmed, except that it means something is growing. Maybe already the heart beats!

The swelling pride, the kicks, the cot. Bibs and rattles accumulating in the spare room, but will I—will we—be ready for this scrap to turn our lives upside down? He'll leave my body, but not my concern, twenty-four hours a day for years on end, with no breaks. In some way I know I'll carry him for the rest of my life, for good or ill.

He could be born whole, or... not. Later he could become damaged by illness, by others, by himself, by me; pray God, not me! He could run a university, a hospice or a marathon, entertain the world, invent the cure for cancer, beat his wife, commit suicide. He could follow God, doing great deeds in his kingdom, or not. He could be my friend for life, or sever all links, except the screaming one in my heart. What have we done?

I want to know. The birth's all pain and risk and hard work. He emerges alien and ugly as some extra-terrestrial; does nothing but yell, redly. But this is a moment to savour for eternity—the wonder of his tiny hands, the sticky warmth of him, his astounding eyes which follow me, whatever the doctors say. He drinks of me, this little one whom our love has gifted with life.

Through laughter and tears, the wonder, pride, humility and devotion chase away all pain. The best baby ever born, I'll protect him with my life. I'll move heaven and earth for him. I'll pick him up when he falls down. I'll run with him. I'll show him all I enjoy, teach him so many things. I'll clear up when he's sick, bandage his grazed knee, wait by his side through pain-filled nights, patch his broken toys and broken confidence when friends betray him. Terrifying thought—it's my love, first, mainly, that will imprint, inform, shape his life.

I'll do my best. I'll comfort him and hold him close, but when the time comes, the hardest thing, I'll let him go—for I want him to grow straight and true, to love others beside me, to make his own choices. Pray God he chooses well—and chooses to include me in his life. And when he hurts me, as he will hurt me, may I keep on trusting him, believing in him, loving him, expecting him to turn back. Though it might be easier to shut off to the possibility of hope, to close off to this hurt a thousand times worse than any pangs of birth, may I keep my heart open, and a welcome ready, always.

> *He found him [his people] in a desert land,*
> *and in the howling waste of the wilderness;*
> *he encircled him, he cared for him,*
> *he kept him as the apple of his eye.*
> *Like an eagle that stirs up its nest,*
> *that flutters over its young, spreading out its wings,*
> *catching them,*
> *bearing them on its pinions.*

Deuteronomy 32:10–11 (RSV)

Meditation

I've always thought of you as Father God, yet your word shows over and over again that you love us like a mother too—you made both father and mother in your image.

Zion will nurse you at her breast,
carry you in her arms,
and hold you in her lap.
I will comfort you there
like a mother
comforting her child.

Isaiah 66:12, 13 (CEV)

A mother feeds and nurtures, is compassionate, intuitive in understanding, tender, firm but comforting; she is always there. I don't live up to that ideal. I've not always put my children before my selfish wants. I've said devastating things to them in anger, or simple irritability. I've not watched over them as I should at times, and given them insufficient rope at others. Impatient, I've yanked them along by the hand, instead of bending down beside them, encouraging them on. I've not always listened, empathized, given time to understand their fears, their conflicts, puzzlements, achievements, hopes and dreams.

My good mother, like all mothers, made mistakes also. Help me to see in contrast that always you have mothered me perfectly and for ever will. Help me to grow past adolescence, to understand a little of the cost of your unflinching devotion, a little of the pain when I trample your love, or throw it back in your face. And then help me to become a child again, safe in the comforting warmth of your arms, knowing that you love me whatever, whenever.

The Lord answered,
'Could a mother forget a child
who nurses at her breast?
Could she fail to love an infant
who came from her own body?
Even if a mother could forget,
I will never forget you.'

Isaiah 49:15 (CEV)

The little girl was dressed in her mother's clothes, the high-heeled shoes ridiculously large, the beads far too long, the skirt held up in one hand— and only a child could have applied make-up like that!

Her voice was bursting with pride, 'Look, mummy, I'm a grown-up lady!' Her mother made all the right noises, but couldn't help smiling at her little girl. And wasn't that God smiling too, seeing both of them as children, with children's needs?

A new-born baby started crying, relentlessly, and never stopped until its need for food was fully satisfied, until it was comfortable and not too hot, until it found the comfort of its mother's hand and breast. And what about us? When we're hungry or in pain or need loving, doesn't God want us to cry out to him, however grown-up we feel? Doesn't he, like the best of mothers, long to supply our every need?

'Children', by Roma Bell

... for you have been my help,
and in the shadow of your wings I sing for joy.

Psalm 63:7

As I meditate on this verse, I can picture myself snuggled so safe and warm under the mother bird's wing that I feel like singing!

I 'see' God's loving face in three different ways. Sometimes he's smiling, as a mother does, holding her young baby. Sometimes it's a listening face, as of one listening to my pain and in some way involved in it. And sometimes it's a transfigured face, like the sun in its strength, shining with personal love for me!

L.D.

The heart of a mother is a deep abyss at the bottom of which you will always discover forgiveness.

Honoré de Balzac (1799–1850)

When God thought of Mother, he must have laughed with satisfaction, and framed it quickly, so rich, so deep, so divine, so full of soul, power and beauty was the conception.

Henry Ward Beecher (1813–87)

Dear Mother: I'm all right. Stop worrying about me.

From an Egyptian papyrus letter
(c. 2000 BC)

It was from you that I first learned to think, to feel, to imagine, to believe.

From a letter to his mother
by John Sterling (1806–44)

GOD'S LOVE AS
A FRIEND

I met her at university, where she was one friend among many. I
noticed her smile, beaming from an open face. Everyone felt more
cheerful when she was around and she brought Christian Union
prayer meetings to life by speaking to God more directly, more
naturally than anyone else.

It was the Easter before my finals when I got to know her better. She invited me to spend a few days with her family, who were
staying in an aunt's holiday house in Wales. After a tussle I decided I needed the break more than the revision—pre-exam tension
was running so high around the campus that I had taken to hiding in my landlady's garden! I was feeling down in other ways too.
Most of my friends had paired off, several were already engaged,
while I, at the advanced age of twenty-one, had given up hope.
The men I liked didn't seem to like me and vice versa!

My friend is the eldest of six. Her father's work forced him to
stay behind so it was her mother, grandmother, four sisters, one
brother and his friend that I met on the train at Shrewsbury. They
had an amazing ability to make me feel as though I was part of the
family right from the start. They even asked for help and advice.
'Chris,' said the mother, in a clothes shop, 'can't you make J. see
sense?' Sister number two had to go to a wedding, but owned
nothing suitable to wear—and the only thing she would try on
now was a fisherman's smock!

We were staying next door to a hill farm, tucked away in a remote valley on the edge of Plynlimon. Relentlessly steep slopes climbed to the top of a waterfall where we stood, gasping for breath, as the snow funnelled upwards into our faces. We returned for hot meals, then to cosy sleeping-bags in a freezing barn-conversion. The wind, the open air, but most of all the friendship blew all my cobwebs away and on the train home I felt human again.

My friend was a year behind me at university, but she married first and they settled, to my delight, in the same church, the same town as myself. A year or so later I married too—and it so happened we bought a house opposite theirs. Her second child and my first were born a month apart and we spent a great deal of time in one another's houses. I learned from her relaxed attitude to babies. Occasionally, when mine screamed non-stop and I felt near breaking point, I scooped him up in a shawl and flopped down with a cup of coffee in her kitchen. I didn't need counselling, parenting classes or intensive prayer, I needed an old friend who'd make me feel normal again and restore my sense of proportion.

You can be yourself with a friend, remove your masks, talk about your deepest worries, your own inadequacies. I valued this particular friend so much because I could be sure of an honest opinion. Sometimes she'd say, 'Chris, that's a dreadful attitude. You can't say or do that!'—and she'd be right. She studied a chapter of my first book in draft form and exclaimed, 'This is about as lively as a learned thesis. Who do you imagine will want to read it?' 'Faithful are the wounds of a friend,' it says in Proverbs, and this proved a most helpful comment! Mostly, though—over and over again—she would encourage me, often literally giving me the courage to 'go for' something. 'Yes, of course you're quite capable of researching that book in Ghana. You'll love it! I'll help look after the kids!'

Inspired by her hospitality and practical creativity, I learnt a great deal from her, but I knew also that I was myself, not her carbon copy. We were good at different things. I valued our differences as well as our similarities; they gave me a fresh perspective on life.

We included others in our friendship, both in the church and outside. We talked through all kinds of issues which concerned us, putting the world, and the church, to rights. We did all kinds of things together, with the children, helping with play-school, going on picnics. In moments of crisis or happiness, she was there and so, I hope, was I, for her.

I've moved away now—different church, different town. We're both so busy that we don't see very much of each other these days. But when we do meet it's just the same, the shared memories, the talking at a deep level, the laughing together. Time passes in a rush, but isn't it great to know that we have all eternity in which to develop friendships!

'Abraham believed God...' and he was called the friend of God.

James 2:23

I do not call you servants any longer, because the servant does not know what the master is doing; but I have called you friends, because I have made known to you everything that I have heard from my Father. You did not choose me but I chose you...

John 15:15–16

Meditation

Real friendships light up your life, but what does it mean that *God* is my friend? That he's for me, certainly. That he likes me and enjoys my company? Can the creator of the universe really be my *friend*? Well, if I think about it I suppose Jesus had friends, plenty of them, and (don't you just love the Bible for being so honest?) they were no more perfect than I am!

People imply it's easy, friendship with God—and that the hard bit is submitting to his Lordship. But a boss/worker relationship is pretty uncomplicated, compared to the richness of friendship, which needs nurturing. Friendship implies a giving and receiving, at peer level—and that's mind-blowing when applied to God.

What can I give to him? Can I encourage him? Is *that* what praise is about?

A friend is someone you talk with, spend time with. You learn together, you do things together—and that means you share memories, happy and sad. Looked at in that way, my friendship with God and his with me can grow and deepen all the time.

But can I be totally honest with him, letting rip, offloading my anger, frustration or bad attitudes, as I do with one or two close friends? Won't he be shocked or reject me? Not if he's my friend. He might rebuke me and set me on the right path again, but that's a different matter. Sometimes he doesn't even need to do that. Once I've offloaded something in his presence my perspective may have changed completely.

True friends normally weather storms and times when they irritate each other because they have invested so much, they're committed, they've become part of one another. A friend includes you in his or her life whether it's convenient or not, whether the house is messy or the kids are ill. And God is the kind of friend who includes others as well. Though I thought my friend's family large, his is infinitely bigger.

Thank you, Lord that you're my friend. I may lose people's friendship, but you will never abandon me—the solid ground of your friendship banishes my fears of the worst excesses of loneliness, no matter what the future might bring. At the best of times no human friend can be with me every moment—in the middle of a long night or when I travel far from home. Thank you that you do remain with me, even though sometimes I feel you're far away. Thank you that you encourage me to pour out my heart to you with total honesty—all the angry and worrying and shameful bits, as well as my joy and thankfulness. Thank you that you accept all my ravings like a huge sheet of blotting-paper and say, 'Having mopped up that lot, shall we be friends again?' Thank you for being the most generous of friends. Help me to enjoy the richness of our friendship more and more. Amen.

Contessina, forgive an old man's babble. But I am your friend, and my love for you goes deep. There is nothing I can give you which you have not got; but there is much, very much, that, while I cannot give it, you can take. No heaven can come to us unless our hearts find rest in it today. Take heaven. No peace lies in the future which is not hidden in this present little instant. Take peace!

The gloom of the world is but a shadow. Behind it, yet within our reach, is joy. There is radiance and glory in the darkness, could we but see; and to see we have only to look. Contessina, I beseech you to look.

Life is so generous a giver, but we, judging its gifts by their covering, cast them away as ugly or heavy or hard. Remove the covering and you will find beneath it a living splendour, woven of love, by wisdom, with power. Welcome it, grasp it, and you touch the angel's hand that brings it to you. Everything we call a trial, a sorrow, or a duty, believe me, that angel's hand is there; the gift is there, and the wonder of an overshadowing presence. Our joys too; be not content with them as joys. They, too, conceal diviner gifts.

Life is so full of meaning and purpose, so full of beauty (beneath its covering) that you will find earth but cloaks your heaven. Courage, then, to claim it; that is all! But courage you have; and the knowledge that we are pilgrims together, wending through unknown country, home.

S.U., a priest (1513)

There was no other way for Love to be
made manifest on earth,
except the way that Love has taken—
the way of birth:

For till Love looks through human eyes,
and lights a human face,
it is not felt by those who live
in Time and Space:

And till Love's lessons had been learnt,
and passed the tests of youth,
how could He tell a waiting world
the words of Truth?

There was no other way by which
He who is Love could reach
the hungry souls, except to heal—
and, healing, teach.

Even today it still is true,
as in each generation,
that Love must manifest anew
by incarnation.

'Love' by Marjorie Noel Williams
(1893–1985)

THE LOVE
OF A SHEPHERD

'Watch out for Amir. I sometimes feel he needs tethering to the nearest responsible adult with a length of elastic!' Mrs Soller had taken me to one side before introducing me to my group for the day. 'Don't look so worried, dear! There's no danger of Samantha and Geeta running off; in fact, they're on the clingy side. I'm afraid they can moan a bit too—need drawing out. Make sure they take an interest in everything and don't let them sulk. As for Daniel, he gets so absorbed in one thing, you may find it hard to move him on to the next.'

I saw what she meant about twenty seconds after we were let loose at the farm. Amir, a silent child, dived off in the wrong direction. 'Amir!' I yelled, running after him, wondering how it was possible for a five-year-old to move so fast, 'Mrs Soller wants our group to see the ducks first.' The teacher had assigned different routes, so that Pink Class would not all crowd around the same pen at once.

I glanced back over my shoulder, concerned about the others. Samantha and Geeta, holding hands, were shuffling uncertainly towards me, eyes wide, mouths drooping. Daniel had remained where I left him, next to the farmyard wall. With a look of angelic concentration on his face, he was poking a stick into the mortar and flicking loose pieces on to the ground.

Mrs Soller had seen my predicament. Scooping up the three stragglers with her arms, she beckoned Amir and me over. 'I've just spoken to the farmer,' she said, 'and d'you know what? One of the ducks' eggs has just hatched. Do you want to be the first to see it?'

The children needed no encouragement from me to run towards the ducks' pen now. Meanwhile Mrs Soller confided, 'Some of the fencing around the pond looks as though it's about to give way. I've had a word with the farmer about it. Steer them clear of that, but, otherwise, have a good day—and don't forget lunch at twelve, under the big tree!'

By lunchtime none of my group had drowned. Nor had they been squashed by the enormous sow which terrified Samantha, so I felt quite pleased with myself. In fact I had lost nothing but my patience. If Mrs Soller managed to control the whole of Pink Class without shouting for terms on end, why couldn't I cope with a small group for a morning? But perhaps I hadn't done so badly. Daniel had refused to look at the animals but was assembling a fine collection of small stones, which proved useful as I could always prevail on him to move to the next pen in search of more. While Amir still wouldn't speak to me, Samantha had held a baby rabbit for the first time—encouraged, I have to say, by the farmer's wife. She had hung back when I suggested it.

By twelve o'clock I was more than ready to sit down and eat my packed lunch with the other mums. We all agreed that looking after four children had worn us to a frazzle and we couldn't imagine how Mrs Soller coped with thirty-four all day. She had taken a double group herself—eight of the most notorious ones, but they seemed all smiles now. She even persuaded Duncan to tell the class about 'What Happened In The Lambing Pen'. All I've ever heard about Duncan is bad news; I didn't realize he had such a sense of humour.

Mrs Soller, looking as fresh as a day-old chick beside the wilting mums, was handing out food to any child who had forgotten to bring some. She'd even brought spare for those whose appetites had quadrupled in the country air.

At the end of the day, she supervised all thirty-four children back on to the coach, dealing out sick-bags to a selected few and peppermints to all. Then she spotted (not one of the parents or Pink Class children had noticed) that one child aboard our coach in fact belonged to another school. The small girl in question gazed up at Mrs Soller with an adoring face. Mrs Soller smiled, put her arm round the girl's shoulders and propelled her firmly off the coach. 'Excuse me for two ticks,' she said to us as she walked down the steps, 'while I sort this out! Now where's that Jessica Ford?' Of course, little Jessica was missing. Not the most popular child in the class, she'd sat by herself on the journey down.

Before we knew it, Mrs Soller had reappeared, carrying a tear-stained Jessica in her arms. The little girl had come running out of the barn as soon as she heard her teacher's voice. 'Would you mind?' Mrs Soller said to the mum who had been sitting beside her. The mum swapped seats and little Jessica snuggled down next to her teacher.

An hour later, as the coach drew up outside the school gates, Mrs Soller gently disentangled herself from the sleeping Jessica. 'Well', she said to everyone, 'thank you, parents. And I think that was a very special day out, don't you, Pink Class?'

> *I am the good shepherd. I know my own and my own know me… And I lay down my life for the sheep.*

John 10:14–15

> *I myself will be the shepherd of my sheep, and I will make them lie down, says the Lord God. I will seek the lost, and I will bring back the strayed, and I will bind up the injured, and I will strengthen the weak, but the fat and the strong I will destroy. I will feed them with justice.*

Ezekiel 34:15–16

Meditation

I've watched them, great flocks of sheep running over the hills. I've noticed how they are drawn in curiosity to anything danger-ous, while remaining foolishly timid about good things, like being led to new pasture. In biblical days the shepherd led his flock from the front—none of this rounding up with dogs. To them his presence meant safety: even the silliest sheep knew that he protected them. He lived with them day and night, and they recognized his voice. When several shepherds penned their flocks together, each sheep distinguished the voice of its own carer and so attached itself to the right person when they emerged to feed the next morning.

See, the Lord God comes with might,
and his arm rules for him;
his reward is with him,
and his recompense before him.
He will feed his flock like a shepherd;
he will gather the lambs in his arms, and carry them in his bosom,
and gently lead the mother sheep.

Isaiah 40:10–11

A shepherd has power over his sheep and the Bible speaks of bad shepherds, who abuse their flock. Thank you, Good Shepherd, that you are strong enough to despatch enemies, but with the sheep themselves you are so gentle. You care not for your own profit but for the weak and vulnerable.

Souls of men! why will ye scatter
Like a crowd of frightened sheep?
Foolish hearts! why will ye wander
From a love so true and deep?

There's a wideness in God's mercy
Like the wideness of the sea;
There's a kindness in his justice
Which is more than liberty.

For the love of God is broader
Than the measures of man's mind;
And the heart of the Eternal
Is most wonderfully kind.

If our love were but more simple,
We should take Him at His word;
And our lives would be all sunshine
In the sweetness of our Lord.

Frederick William Faber (1814–63)

THE LOVE OF A RESTORER OR GARDENER

This bare patch of ground—dry, dusty, strewn with stones—is hardly the place to start a garden. Yet he toils here in the sun, taking no account of his own thirst, caring only for the needs of the plants, the little seedlings he's trying to grow. Delicate, they wilt. After a few days most seem to have given up the struggle for life, but he goes on tending them. He brings them water, not in a deluge, but carefully, a drop at a time, and only when the sun is low enough not to scorch. In the heat of the day he digs deep, through earth baked like concrete in the sun. Always he excavates holes far larger than these tiny plants need and then he's to and fro with his wheelbarrow, bringing in compost and good topsoil. That must come at a price in these parts. Desert plants have never had it so good! Finally, he lays grit to keep the moisture in.

He creates protection too, fences of sticks bound together. The dust storms which whip across these plains, choking every living thing, will spend their fury on something other than his precious seedlings. Any beast, lost and starving in this wilderness, will be hard pushed to devour or trample this garden.

And his efforts are beginning to show results. Many of the plants are perking up, sending out shoots. One or two have even flowered. To see blues and purples and so many shades of green in this desert lifts my heart. Here each plant, however common elsewhere, seems like a gift from heaven.

He's working still, planning—and diverting far-off streams to flow in this direction. Ambitious, he's after no tiny square of a garden but a whole estate, as though determined that the whole desert shall bloom. Imagine it—fields of waving grasses and poppies, with yellow mulleins towering like candelabras and tiny, perfect desert roses; with acacia and mimosa and tall cypress trees giving shape and perfuming every season!

See the old hut over there? He's been working on that too. Since the sheep ate all that grew here and the shepherds moved on, generations ago, its tumble-down stones have served as a landmark in this place. Its forlorn ruin symbolizes the spot where hope died. Yet he has been gathering its scattered stones together, fitting them carefully one on top of another. I've seen him carrying palm branches to thatch its roof again. I think he's almost finished now. Perhaps people will live here again—and why not? With food and water and this rare beauty to sustain them, they would have everything they need. He has placed a mug full of flowers in the open doorway, as if to welcome strangers, and my nose tickles at their sharp scent, carried on the wind.

The poor and needy seek water, but there is none, their tongues fail for thirst. I, the Lord, will hear them; I, the God of Israel, will not forsake them.
I will open rivers in desolate heights, and fountains in the midst of the valleys; I will make the wilderness a pool of water, and the dry land springs of water.
I will plant in the wilderness the cedar and the acacia tree, the myrtle and the oil tree; I will set in the desert the cypress tree and the pine and the box tree together,
That they may see and know, and consider and understand together, that the hand of the Lord has done this, and the Holy One of Israel has created it.

Isaiah 41:17–20 (NKJ)

Meditation

When sudden clouds deluge the desert with water, once every decade or so, seeds which have lain dry and dormant grow and flower in record time. The wild flower meadow which springs up seems all the more lovely for its rarity.

Thank you, Lord, that my dryness is no problem to you, since the water of your love can bring me to life again. Thank you that the most careful restorer of ancient artefacts comes nowhere near you in skill and tenderness, as you piece together our brokenness—for to you we're always worth the pains, the care!

To console those who mourn in Zion, to give them beauty for ashes,
the oil of joy for mourning, the garment of praise for the spirit of
heaviness; that they may be called trees of righteousness, the planting
of the Lord, that he may be glorified.
And they shall rebuild the old ruins, they shall raise up the former
desolations, and they shall repair the ruined cities,
the desolations of many generations.

Isaiah 61:3–4 (NKJ)

I'm fragile like a rose,
Petals torn, feelings hung
By bare threads of emotion,
Reaching out for love and assurance.

Fragile like a rose,
Each tender leaf stripped bare,
Devoid of nourishment,
Gasping for breath of life.

Fragile like a rose,
Each thorn intact,
Scarring deep the hand
Which reaches out to care.

Fragile like a rose,
And yet nothing to show for beauty,
But loneliness and scarcely a will
To go on, but persisting.

Fragile like a rose,
In rays of morning sunshine,
Surrounding each leaf,
Touching each petal,
Bringing glory through the dark.

'The Love of God', by Janine Madge

How fresh, O Lord, how sweet and clean
Are thy returns! ev'n as the flowers in spring;
To which, besides their own demean,
The late-past frosts tributes of pleasures bring.
Grief melts away
Like snow in May,
As if there were no such cold thing.

Who would have thought my shrivel'd heart
Could have recover'd greenness? It was gone
Quite under ground; as flowers depart
To see their mother-root, when they have blown;
Where they together
All the hard weather,
Dead to the world, keep house unknown.

From 'The Flower', by George Herbert
(1593–1632)

THE LOVE OF AN ARTIST
FOR HIS CREATION

For goodness' sake, wouldn't a flat-pack have done? They're not bad, the ones down at the DIY store. I've seen one or two I wouldn't mind at all. Anyway, it's going to be covered by a tablecloth most of the time. What's the point of going to all this trouble?

Yes, you're right, I am fed up with the mess—and the noise. It's been six weeks now. This room's unusable and the dust from all that sanding and planing gets into every corner of the house. OK, you have helped clear it up a few times, thank you very much!

But have a think, before you get taken with the urge to make some more furniture. Those flat-packs come with nice clear instructions—none of this going out buying expensive hardwood and hoping you've got the design right. With flat-packs, if the manufacturer cuts it wrong, that's their problem; they'd have to take it back! But normally it's fine. You screw the bits together, apply a few spots of glue and it's all ready in half an hour. It saves no end of time and stress, as well as money.

So what if there would be thousands of identical ones? Look, I'm not being rude, but your table's dead simple, isn't it? If you were into marquetry or something I could see the point of all these hours of craftsmanship. But the only reason it's taken you all this time is that you refuse to use power tools. Whoever heard of someone sanding by hand these days, apart from the finishing touches?

Yes, I'll grant that you've used the grain beautifully and I guess you could photograph those joints and use them in a textbook on cabinet making, but guests aren't going to crawl under the table looking at them, are they?

OK, so the joints are strong and you find good workmanship pleasing. I know what you mean. I get a good deal of pleasure out of my little watercolour sketches, or from preparing a really special meal, but this is in a different league. I must say you have far more patience than me.

Yes, of course I've heard of the Amish. I know they made simple things with loving care. Worth a fortune, their furniture is. Oh, I see, thought you'd follow in their footsteps, did you? Crafty!

It's not about making money? I might have known. You simply enjoy making good, plain, honest furniture, as beautifully as you can? Honestly, I give up!

> ... we are the clay, and you are our potter;
> we are all the work of your hand.

> Isaiah 64:8

Meditation

Sometimes, Lord, I think it would be great if you used moulds. You could get some of that liquid clay stuff, pour it in, let it set and there we'd be, lots of nice Christians, all praising you and loving each other and doing good. We wouldn't have to be exactly the same; you could have different moulds—different sizes, different shapes, special ones with twiddly bits (so long as they weren't so elaborate you'd risk breaking the pot when you took the mould away). You could even colour the clay mixture before pouring it in. You can get brilliant effects like that, or so I've heard.

The thing is, Lord, I'm not too keen on being thrown on the wheel. It makes me so dizzy and when you dig your thumbs in, it hurts. Yes, I know you use that nice warm, lubricating water of the Holy Spirit and I'm really grateful, but I do feel that the mould method would be less stressful all round, really. If you want my opinion, that is.

No, you're right, the pot shouldn't tell the potter what to do. I'm really sorry. And yes, I do see that this way I will be unique. But—forgive me, Lord, can I say that, at the moment, I seem to be coming out a bit of an odd shape? It's just that if I go all askew—and I've seen that happen to clay on the potter's wheel before now—what happens then? I can't help noticing that bin over there out of the corner of my eye as I'm whizzing round.

Oh, that's a relief! You never throw us away, you start again! No, I don't suppose that would be possible with the mould method, not once it was hard and dry. And yes, I do appreciate that this way I have your personal attention.

No, I can't say I had realized that you take pride and pleasure in me, even now, before I'm completed. I'm a masterpiece in the making? Me? Go on!

Yes, I understand now. You're a true craftsman, producing nothing but masterpieces. No, they don't come cheap, whatever way you look at it. You can say that again, Lord!

Ouch, is that pinching really necessary? OK, OK. You're the boss. Do what you have to do! Oh and, by the way, thanks for taking so much trouble!

> For it was you who formed my inward parts;
> you knit me together in my mother's womb.
> I praise you, for I am fearfully and wonderfully made.
> Wonderful are your works; that I know very well.

Psalm 139:13–14

> What heart could have thought you?—
> Past our devisal
> (O filigree petal!)
> Fashioned so purely,
> Fragilely, surely,
> From what Paradisal
> Imagineless metal,
> Too costly for cost?
> Who hammered you, wrought you,
> From argentine vapour?—

'God was my shaper.
Passing surmisal,
He hammered, He wrought me,
From curled silver vapour,
To lust of His mind:—
Thou could'st not have thought me!
So purely, so palely,
Tinily, surely,
Mightily, frailly,
Insculped and embossed,
With His hammer of wind,
And His graver of frost.'

'To a Snowflake',
by Francis Thompson (1859–1907)

How should I praise thee, Lord! how should my rhymes
Gladly engrave thy love in steel,
If what my soul doth feel sometimes,
My soul might ever feel!

Although there were some forty heavens, or more,
Sometimes I peer above them all;
Sometimes I hardly reach a score,
Sometimes to hell I fall.

O rack me not to such a vast extent;
Those distances belong to thee:
The world's too little for thy tent,
A grave too big for me.

Wilt thou meet arms with man, that thou dost stretch
A crumb of dust from heaven to hell?
Will great God measure with a wretch?
Shall he thy stature spell?

O let me, when thy roof my soul hath hid,
O let me roost and nestle there:
Then of a sinner thou art rid,
And I of hope and fear.

Yet take thy way; for sure thy way is best:
Stretch or contract me, thy poor debtor:
This is but tuning of my breast,
To make the music better.

Whether I fly with angels, fall with dust,
Thy hands made both, and I am there:
Thy power and love, my love and trust
Make one place everywhere.

'The Temper', by George Herbert
(1593–1633)

A LOVER'S PASSION

Don't be shy! I can see you, even though you imagine you're hiding. Your beauty shines out among the dark rocks of that forbidding cliff face as jewels sparkle from the black hair of a princess. You have no need to hide as a stratagem to intrigue me, for my thoughts are with you all the day long.

Those rocks can't shield your beauty from my eyes, and yet the cliff face holds dangers for you, so don't be shy. Come here to me. I want to hear you sing; I want to hold you tight and feast upon your beauty. Don't flinch; I will not devour you. Have you not heard of the feast of legend, which renews itself as fast as it is enjoyed? Love is like that. My passion for you is like the burning bush which is never consumed, never fizzles out in a wisp of smoke and pile of grey ash. My passion burns and leaps; it crackles incandescent; its flames have lit the world since before time began and they will never be extinguished.

Little white dove, you turn your face away from the heat of my passion, fearing impropriety. Don't you know that gold, to be refined, must melt white in the furnace? Its abandonment to a greater power purifies it. Lovers who look on one another's nakedness are not ashamed. In the fertile soil of intimacy, seeing all, knowing all, their passion grows, flowers, fruits. I want to know you, your inmost being, the parts you hide, even from yourself. Already I have done as much for you! I gave all, risked all for you, enduring mockery as I hung naked, chose to stay there, defenceless for you, so that there should be nothing between us, not the barrier of the least thought.

That pain is past. This is springtime and I know that I have won your heart. Sing to me; sing freely from your spirit, from the depths of your being. No, I don't hear croaks and wobbles; I love to hear you sing. Listen, understand me, I'm not flattering you—I really do delight to hear your voice. Sing again, my darling!

My love, come closer. I can see that you feel vulnerable, but I want to please you; I want to hear you cry out in ecstasy at my touch. My passion will transform you—it's those who feel my passion who change the world with me, who blast away the jagged rocks and light the landscape with lamps of multiplying love.

O my dove, in the clefts of the rock,
in the covert of the cliff,
let me see your face,
let me hear your voice;
for your voice is sweet,
and your face is lovely...

I slept, but my heart was awake.
Listen! My beloved is knocking.
'Open to me, my sister, my love,
my dove, my perfect one;
for my head is wet with dew,
my locks with the drops of the night.'
I had put off my garment;
how could I put it on again?
I had bathed my feet;
how could I soil them?
My beloved thrust his hand into the opening,
and my inmost being yearned for him.
I arose to open to my beloved,
and my hands dripped with myrrh,
my fingers with liquid myrrh,
upon the handles of the bolt.
I opened to my beloved,
but my beloved had turned and was gone...

Song of Solomon 2:14; 5:2–6

Meditation

Sometimes the intensity of your passion frightens me, Lord. Though the Bible is full of imagery of you as a bridegroom, I don't find it easy to think of you in that way and find myself holding back. Sometimes you withdraw your presence, causing me to search for you in desperation, as the Beloved did in that ancient poem. She was willing to go anywhere, do anything to find her lover. He was not fickle. Once she admitted how much he meant to her, once she had searched all night, she found him again, pasturing his flock among the lilies.

Lord, help me not to run and hide from you because I feel unworthy, when you have proved once and for all that you love me and want me close to you. Help me to expose myself to the full blast of your passion, over and over again, so that it fills and expands me to the limit and beyond, making my life, my actions, one with yours.

Me, Lord? Canst thou mispend
One word, misplace one look on me?
Call'st me thy Love, thy Friend?
Can this poor soul the object be
Of these love-glances, those life-kindling eyes?
What? I the centre of thy arms' embraces?
Of all thy labour I the prize?
Love never mocks, truth never lies.
Oh how I quake: Hope fear, fear hope displaces:
I would, but cannot hope: such wondrous love amazes.

From 'The Divine Lover'
by Phineas Fletcher (1582–1650)

It is said that when [the turtle-dove] cannot find its mate it will not sit on any green bough, or drink cool refreshing water, nor rest in the shade, nor mingle with its companions. But when it finds its mate it does all these things.

Such too must be the soul if it is to attain union with the Bridegroom. The soul's love and anxiety must be such that it cannot rest on the green boughs of any joy, nor drink the waters of the world's honour and glory, nor shelter in the shade of created help and protection. It must mourn in its loneliness until it finds the Bridegroom to its heart's content.

'The Dove' by St John of the Cross
(1542–91)

THE LOVE OF A HUSBAND

He fell in love with me—with me! He could have chosen anyone.
Foreign princesses, glittering daughters of wealthy men would
have slogged around the world, done anything; but he chose me;
he wooed me! He ran after me, as though intoxicated, saying such
extravagant things, giving me presents, taking me to places where
I never would have dreamed of going. He fixed all his attention on
me! My heart raced when he came near, my breath came shallow.
I told myself again and again not to hope—that tomorrow his eye
would fall on someone else. But now I know that his heart beat
faster and more strongly than mine. He told me, later, how
thoughts of me kept him awake at night; how, by day, he'd think
he'd caught sight of my hair in a crowd, or he would smell lilies
and leave everything to go running after me. Yet I had no long
hours to spend curling my hair and cosseting my skin; I could
afford no fine perfume.

So, for a long time, I wouldn't believe him. It took an age to
convince me that he would love me like this always, that he would
marry me, binding himself to me in faithfulness, with no going
back. Kings' sons are known for passing infatuations, or else for a
certain condescension and stiff duty. No wonder I found it hard to
believe in his kindness! But he spoke words of comfort each time
I needed them; he seemed to understand the very heart of me.
Before I met him, I was trapped in a ravine of trouble, whose walls
I could never hope to scale, whose end I could never hope to

reach. I had no hope—but he gave me hope. After a while I began to think that if he, so wise and good, saw something special in me, who was I to call him a liar? Once I dared to believe that his love for me was genuine, I learnt to trust that he would not pick me up only to drop me down the cliff face. Then he lifted me into a wide place, full of good things.

Our marriage hasn't been all happy ever after, of course. We've had our disagreements from time to time and I've balked at some of the decisions he's taken—and yet he's always loved me for who I am, that's the wonder of it. He's always cared for me, considered my feelings, wanted the best for me... and not many women can say that of their husbands, not after all these years. I must admit that I take him for granted sometimes. Yet still he surprises me with the freshness of his love, showing me through word and touch and look and deed that he values me as much as ever. I wasted so much time misinterpreting his delight in me for a mistake or a passing infatuation. Now I've proof that his deep passion is a strong under-current which drives his being. It carries me along, always giving far more than it takes—and I'm so grateful, so very grateful! All I can do is to love, delight in and honour him in return.

My bride, my very own, you have stolen my heart!
With one glance from your eyes
and the glow of your necklace,
you have stolen my heart.
Your love is sweeter than wine;
the smell of your perfume
is more fragrant than spices.

Song of Solomon 4:9–10 (CEV)

Meditation

I pasted the following words by Tricia Richards in the front of my prayer diary and look at them often before I pray:

'We need to spend some time together, you and I. Oh I know you are always busy—but I miss you. There was a time when a moment in my arms would leave you breathless and in a whirl—but that moment becomes an intrusion on your busy schedule.

'What happened? How did our relationship become so passé and bland? Your heart would miss a beat when I surprised you with my presence and time together was not dulled by necessity or predictability.

'It's not as though you don't love me any more, because I know you do—you forget I know you so well. It takes time and effort—oh I don't mean the drudgery and going over familiar ground—I mean taking a step back, listening, making time to listen. Tell me about your day, I want to know. Do not assume that, because we know each other well, you do not need to talk to me; tell me your thoughts, your feelings, your hopes and your doubts. Do not allow our love to become bland, predictable, accepting it as it is. Remember how it was at first—we are so much further on now, you and I. We can be more intimate, more open—trust me more. For you I have been broken-hearted, for you I have been wounded, for you I have been patient, strong and loyal. For you I have love; I have not changed.

'Do not be robbed by the great pretender. Pretence only breeds disillusionment. So let us be honest and you will find I am the same. Let me once again be your first love. It is not in doing but in being.'

Tricia Richards

Therefore, behold, I will allure her, will bring her into the wilderness, and speak comfort to her. I will give her her vineyards from there, and the Valley of Achor [trouble] as a door of hope; she shall sing there, as in the days of her youth, as in the day when she came up from the land of Egypt... I will betroth you to Me forever; yes, I will betroth you to Me in righteousness and justice, in lovingkindness and mercy; I will betroth you to Me in faithfulness, and you shall know the Lord.

Hosea 2:14–15, 19–20 (NKJ)

A great cry in the ears of God is this burning affection of the spirit, which saith: My God thou art my Love: thou art all mine and I am all thine. Enlarge me in love, that I may learn to taste with the inner mouth of the heart how sweet it is to love and to be melted and to swim in love.

Let me be possessed by Love, and lifted out of myself in the fervour of ecstasy.

I will sing the song of Love, I will follow thee, my Beloved, on high: my soul shall grow faint in thy praise, exulting in love.

From 'The Imitation of Christ',
by Thomas à Kempis (1379–1471)

Jesus, I am resting, resting in the joy of what thou art;
I am finding out the greatness of thy loving heart.
Thou hast bid me gaze upon thee, and thy beauty fills my soul,
For by thy transforming power thou hast made me whole.

Oh, how great thy loving-kindness, vaster, broader than the sea!
Oh, how marvellous thy goodness, lavished all on me!
Yes, I rest in thee, Beloved, know what wealth of grace is thine,
Know thy certainty of promise, and have made it mine.

Simply trusting thee, Lord Jesus, I behold thee as thou art;
And thy love so pure, so changeless, satisfies my heart:
Satisfies its deepest longings, meets, supplies its every need,
Compasseth me round with blessings; thine is love indeed!

From 'Jesus, I am resting, resting',
by Jean Sophia Pigott (1845–82)

HIS LOVE SHOWN TO US THROUGH OTHERS

I see your face, Lord, in the love of people. Sometimes they, like me, make mistakes or aren't very loving. But there again, I see so many little acts of kindness, of consideration, of remembrance or practical care. I see you when someone shares their vulnerability, is lost in worship, or prays, with halting words, from some deep place within; when someone is willing to laugh like a child with me, or makes real efforts to include the lonely and marginalized among their friends.

When I'm in distress, when I cry and scream, sometimes you come direct, wrapping me in your peace that passes understanding and with your warm blanket of love which makes me feel secure. But normally I won't stay still for long enough. You know me well, you know my writhings need the touch of a human hand; the wild churnings of my brain will calm only to a human voice. And so you send a friend. Most often you seem to choose the one I would never think of looking for. Trusted friends may have let me down, caused my pain, even. Perhaps the one I turn to is simply not at home. Unable to wait, I shout some incoherent gibberish at you, a 'Mayday' call for help, then the phone rings, or the door. One not from my community or church or theology even, one I haven't seen for years—or haven't met before, perhaps—is there and gifts me with time and full attention. The friend listens, brings comfort, wisdom, laughter, shares my load, helps restore my sense of proportion, makes me feel whole and human again.

I don't deserve this, Lord—this reassuring hug you send from heaven through your best-loved here on earth. You know my faith is little, that I crave to feel the evidence of your love in the flesh—like Thomas, to see with my eyes and touch with my hands. Let me not forget these hugs of yours, though the details may be small and the crises long ago passed. I will celebrate—the timing, the detail, the 'coincidences'—all the warm proofs of your care. And I'll try to remember those things next time I doubt you.

Another thing, Lord—I was thinking how sometimes, unknowingly, I've found myself the one you've sent to hug another of your children. My presence somehow brought your resources into the situation and changed it around, though I never dreamed I did much at the time. May I stay sensitive—however unexpected, however strange the time and situation. May I stay available to be your love to others. May I love them as you have loved me.

... love one another as I have loved you.

John 15:12

Freely you have received, freely give.

Matthew 10:8 (NKJ)

Meditation

It would be a strange, bloated kind of person who received love all the time, from God or from people, and never gave any back. It is in giving that we receive, very often, but before we can give something, we must own it first. We can only give love if we have first received love—psychologists and the Bible agree on that! God's love for us comes first. It's the foundation for all other love.

We can only love him because he first loved us. People, as well as inspiring us to love, may let us down. God's love won't, even though we may not always *feel* loved by him. Those who follow his ways often see his love triumph in the grimmest of circumstances.

Time magazine called Robert Coles 'the most influential living psychiatrist in the US'. He won a Pulitzer prize for his book *Children of Crisis*. Coles came to faith largely because of a six-year-old black child from a deprived family. Her name was Ruby Bridges and she caused a major racial disturbance every day as she went to school. She was the first black child to attend Frantz Elementary School in New Orleans and the other students boycotted it because of her. Each morning troops closed off roads, while federal marshals led little Ruby through a wild crowd of swearing, shouting, angry people.

Horrified, Coles decided to help Ruby and her family, but instead she changed his life. According to all the theories, she should have suffered major psychological damage, but he found she prayed each day that God would take away her fear and help her to forgive these people. 'Because that's what Jesus did on the Cross,' was all she said in explanation. Previously Coles had thought such high moral ground might be attained by a few saintly individuals after years and years of discipline, but never by a poor six-year-old with no education or real example to follow.

From the source of all love, Ruby drew enough to give and give again. In giving, and forgiving, she received not hurt and bitterness but strength and an ability to hold her head high—to live as a happy child despite everything. She challenged Coles; she challenges me. God's love is real. It makes a difference. It makes all the difference.

Lord, make me an instrument of Thy peace.
Where there is hatred, let me sow love;
Where there is injury, pardon;
Where there is doubt, faith;
Where there is despair, hope;
Where there is darkness, light;
Where there is sadness, joy.

O Divine Master, grant that I may not so much seek
To be consoled as to console;
Not so much to be understood as to understand;
Not so much to be loved as to love:
For it is in giving that we receive;
It is in pardoning that we are pardoned;
It is in dying that we awaken to eternal life.

Francis of Assisi (1182–1226)

He's engrossed in simultaneous translation.
The language I cannot understand—
Mouth forming words with no voice,
Hands a blur of movement.
But his face speaks!
None so deaf who cannot hear his spirited
Body language, spanning the silent world and mine.
Laughter and hope in his eyes,
Friendly, bridging the gulf
Between two cultures,
Two worlds.
Like the African
Who once put a sermon
From her language into mine—
Truths that I'd heard many times
So lived and sparkled in her eyes
They tongued her words with fire.
And when she spoke of Jesus' love,
Small muscles creased
Her dark skin into a smile.
We sat beyond time and place and race
Windowing heaven.

'Sign Language', by Christine Leonard

A tiny boy
came dancing up to me,
his brown face bright with smiles, and beaming
with the love of living.
He was holding out a spray
of cherry blossom he had found
upon the ground.
'How beautiful!' I tried to say,
'Are you taking it to Mother?'
But he did not understand,
for he was from Brazil, and knew
no English yet.

My friend discovered what he meant,
and said, 'He's giving it to you.'
I took it from his hand,
and smiled my thanks,
and he ran home, content.

What inward guardian told
that child, just four years old
about the joy of giving?
I shall not soon forget
that little foreigner who found his pleasure
in offering me, so old,
his latest treasure.

From 'Surprise Gift', by Marjorie Noel
Williams (1893–1985)

ULTIMATE LOVE

It's a bloody mess! All those promises, all those dreams—he had such life and energy about him and, what would you call it? Nobility? Authority? Some of us even thought you'd call it divinity. We were all convinced that he was unique, that he was going to change the world—and that we'd have a front seat view!

But it's come to this—to bloody flesh, to a dead body of less use than a slab of meat. We thought he had such a special touch, drawing good out of people, getting them to change their lives and follow him—to what? To this?

It's ironic. He was always confounding our imaginations by turning around the most hopeless scenarios. When he arrived in town, those who'd been lame or blind from birth ended up dancing down the streets. He played havoc with other people's funerals too, but that's all over now. It's pay-back time. I suppose we assumed he'd always deal with the opposition, no trouble. He'd always known exactly what to do and say before. But yesterday all the hatred and evil in the world seemed to rear up against him—and won. Even the sky turned black.

More fool us, the beautiful bubble's burst and our world has come to an end. Yes, of course we're scared—terrified. That wasn't the only reason most of us ran away, though. Well, could *you* have borne to watch the extremes of his agony, his shame? Not if you'd known him as well as we did, I'll bet.

The crowd did a complete about-face. They looked on jeering. We had thought some of them were beginning to believe that he would save us—and not just from our oppressors. They seemed to sense that he had some divine spark. He would save us from ourselves and take us back to a time when everyone wanted, more than they wanted anything else in the world, to love God and to love one another. In hindsight, of course, it was all too good to be true. It was utter foolishness—what ever made us think that any god would come to this stinking place to help us? What god would choose to leave a paradise of eternal bliss to come here and tramp around the dusty countryside? No god has ever decided to spend years with people who were never really going to understand him. And most certainly no god would come here to suffer and die—never has and never will.

And yet... I still can't really believe that he has gone.

> *... unless you eat the flesh of the Son of Man and drink his blood, you have no life in you.*
>
> John 6:53

Meditation

Your love, taken to its ultimate extreme, is hardly cosy and warm. I find it stark, shocking. Sometimes I wear a little silver cross around my neck—a strange thing to do, since it symbolizes an instrument of torture. As well as being our narrow gateway to salvation, the cross has proved a stumbling-block ever since Jesus told some Jews, of all people, that their lives depended on eating his flesh and drinking his blood. The depth of his passion, the awfulness of it, is not something I care to examine too closely, and when I come within a mile it brings me to my knees. But I suppose that nothing less powerful could change the rules and issue in a new era, a new covenant, a new start.

> *He was despised and rejected by others;*
> *a man of suffering and acquainted with infirmity;*
> *and as one from whom others hide their faces*
> *he was despised, and we held him of no account.*

Surely he has borne our infirmities
and carried our diseases;
yet we accounted him stricken, struck down by God, and afflicted.
But he was wounded for our transgressions,
crushed for our iniquities;
upon him was the punishment that made us whole,
and by his bruises we are healed.

Isaiah 53:3–5

Jesus, one reason we can't feel your love as we ought is the scar tissue we bear from the times when we've been rejected by people, maybe the very people we might have expected to love us. Even the most happy and secure of us have suffered rejection at some time in our lives and know its power to shrivel us up. Yet you willingly accepted rejection of the worst kind, rejection by your Father. When you took all my filth and evil on you, the holy God had to turn away, leaving you to that terrible death, that scorn, that shame, that utter desertion. You in turn gave me all your goodness, so that I became pure in Father's eyes. How can I ever thank you? How can I ever understand the depths of your love and the risks you took for me? Or that you, Father, gave what you valued most in order to reconcile this world with yourself, when it was we who broke the harmony in the first place.

. . . looking to Jesus the pioneer and perfecter of our faith, who for the
sake of the joy that was set before him endured the cross, disregarding
its shame, and has taken his seat at the right hand
of the throne of God.

Hebrews 12:2

This verse amazes me, Lord, when I think, what *was* the joy that was set before you? It wasn't heaven—that's where you came from. You could have stayed there, in unending bliss, with your dear Father and the Holy Spirit. With them you could have reigned serene over the universe, once you'd wiped out the pathetic inhabitants of that troublesome little planet, Earth. So what was the joy that was set before you, the joy so great that you felt no shame, despite hanging naked on a cross, despite being mocked and tortured by your own creations? What did you gain by it? I can't think of anything except for a relationship with us! Our sin had got in the way before. To think that knowing us, knowing me, causes you joy like that—joy which motivated you to endure the cross!

And now you've finished. Our sin's dealt with. You sit there at the right hand of the throne of God and to everyone who cries out, 'Help me, forgive me,' you reach out your hand and say, 'I've been through so much to get to know you. Come, sit here beside me and tell me all about yourself!'

Someone said that Christ drank the cup of bitterness and separation so that we might have the wine of communion. *Take, eat— this is my body, which is given for you! This cup is the new covenant in my blood.*

> Most glorious Lord of life, that on this day
> Didst make thy triumph over death and sin;
> And having harrow'd hell didst bring away
> Captivity thence captive, us to win:
> This joyous day, dear Lord, with joy begin,
> And grant that we for whom thou didest die,
> Being with thy dear blood clean washed from sin,
> May live forever in felicity.
> And that thy love we weighing worthily,
> May likewise love thee for the same again;
> And for thy sake that all like dear didst buy,
> With love may one another entertain.
> So let us love, dear love, like as we ought.
> Love is the lesson which the Lord us taught.

'Easter Sonnet' by Edmund Spenser
(1552–99)

My song is love unknown,
My Saviour's love to me,
Love to the loveless shown,
That they might lovely be.
O who am I,
That for my sake
My Lord should take frail flesh, and die?

He came from his blest throne,
Salvation to bestow;
But men made strange, and none
The longed-for Christ would know;
But O, my Friend,
My Friend indeed,
Who at my need his life did spend!

In life, no house, no home
My Lord on earth might have;
In death, no friendly tomb
But what a stranger gave.
What may I say?
Heaven was his home;
But mine the tomb wherein he lay.

From 'My Song is Love Unknown', by
Samuel Crossman (1624–83)

LOVE FOR THE UNDERDOG

There she goes, making the ground shake. You can't help laughing at that galumphing run. She certainly wouldn't win a prize as a ballet dancer, nor in a beauty competition. I'd envy those huge eyes and luscious eyelashes on anyone else, yet on her they manage to look ridiculous. I guess it's because of her long, straggly neck and that enormous beak, to say nothing of her tree-trunk thighs. As for that ridiculous plumage, of which she's so proud, have you ever seen anything so overdone!

And what's she famous for? Hiding her head in the sand! She's all enthusiasm and curiosity and boundless energy, like a kittenish kick-boxer—until it comes to the crunch and then, well, she's no idea what to do!

Look at the size of her head. Isn't it tiny when compared with her body? You can tell by that alone that she's no mastermind at the best of times! Not much room for brains in that skull, poor dear. I mean to say, other animals, even primitive ones, manage to care for their young incredibly well for years at a time, but what does she do? Lays her eggs on the ground and simply leaves them there, where anyone could tread on them—or eat them, come to that. She seems to have no idea of priorities, poor thing—no common sense whatsoever.

She reminds me of... well, I won't mention any names. Everyone knows some feckless, happy-go-lucky types, who spend their lives being rescued by everyone else, yet still manage to think they're the bee's knees.

Oh. Yes, all right Lord. I suppose you did make the ostrich, but, to be honest, I can't help feeling that she wasn't one of your better ideas. Good for a laugh, but... What's that? The ostrich is challenging *me*? To a race? Well, er, yes, obviously she can outrun me—look at those legs, I mean it's hardly fair... You'll supply a horse for me to ride on? Ah. Um, if you'll excuse me, I'm just off to bury my head in a nice bit of sand...!

An ostrich proudly flaps her wings,
but not because she loves her young.
She abandons her eggs
and lets the dusty ground keep them warm.
And she doesn't seem to worry
that the feet of an animal could crush them all.
She treats her eggs as though they were not her own,
unconcerned that her work might be for nothing.
I myself made her foolish and without common sense.
But once she starts running,
she laughs at a rider on the fastest horse.

Job 39:13–18 (CEV)

Meditation

Thank you, Lord, that your love works overtime, bringing out the best in all of us 'underdogs', whether we resemble ostriches, three-toed sloths or silly sheep. When you laugh at us (because we *are* funny) it's with deep affection. And, it seems, the more foolish we are, the less we have, the more you choose to trust and use us to bring about your good purposes. Your ways are certainly not our ways. You keep turning our thinking upside-down as you go out of your way to bless the poor in spirit, the meek, the hated, those who have lost everything. You're the original radical, acting not out of cold ideology but love. You really do love ostriches and you appreciate each one of us humans too. However daft we seem to ourselves, however much anyone or everyone else thinks we're total failures, fit only for the rubbish bin, to you we're more than trusted co-workers; we're stars.

The Lord has used his powerful arm
to scatter those who are proud.
He drags strong rulers from their thrones
and puts humble people in places of power.
God gives the hungry good things to eat,
and sends the rich away with nothing.

Luke 1:51–53 (CEV)

My dear friends, remember what you were when God chose you. The
people of this world didn't think that many of you were wise. Only a
few of you were in places of power, and not many of you came from
important families. But God chose the foolish things of this world to
put the wise to shame. He chose the weak things of this world to put
the powerful to shame. What the world thinks is worthless, useless, and
nothing at all is what God has used to destroy what the world
considers important.

1 Corinthians 1:26–28 (CEV)

And I smiled to think God's greatness flowed
Around our incompleteness;
Round our restlessness, His rest.

From 'Rime of the Duchess May',
by Elizabeth Barrett Browning (1806–61)

'How can I love you, Lord?' I asked. He answered, 'Be aware of your sins and of my love. Do not be afraid, what a person has been in the past is not important, what matters is what they will be in the future. Remember Mary Magdalene, St Paul and many other saints, before they knew me. The dishonest I make honest, the bad I make good.'

Margery Kempe (1373–?)

God can make himself known only through those works of his which he reveals in us, which we feel and experience within ourselves. When the experience is to learn that he is a God who looks into the depths and helps principally the poor, despised, afflicted, miserable, forsaken and those who are of no account, at that very moment a love for him is created and surges up from the heart's core. The heart overflows with gladness, and leaps and dances for the joy it has found in God.

Martin Luther (1483–1546)

The Church do seem a touching sight,
When folk a-coming in at door
Do softly tread the long-aisled floor
Below the pillared arches' height,
With bells a-pealing,
Folk a-kneeling,
Heart a-healing, wi' the love
An' peace a-sent 'em from above.

And there, wi' mild an' thoughtful face,
Wi' down-cast eyes and voices dumb,
The old and young do slowly come
And take in stillness each his place;
A-sinking slowly
Kneeling lowly,
Seeking holy thoughts alone
In prayer before their Maker's throne.

'In Church', by William Barnes
(1800–86)

AN UNCOMPROMISING LOVE

It snowed last night. This morning, spring sunshine has melted most of it, leaving wet roads and a sodden landscape. But high on the wide hills some remains, marking those places where last night the drifts lay deep. Snowy white lines trace farm tracks up north-facing hills. The tangly growth under each hedge lies beneath layers of smooth, cold whiteness.

I find myself wondering why these landscape 'highlights' startle and unsettle me. Then I see—it's as though an artist, refusing to paint the shadows, has left the paper blank. I understand how someone would be reluctant to examine rutted tracks filled with enough mire to pull your boot off and containing... let's not think about it! The snow has piled against the base of that decaying post—the kind of place where a dog might lift its leg, a thorny shelter for rank nettles and nameless creeping things. How innocent it looks now!

The low winter sun dazzles. It's hard for anyone, painting against the light. Your eyes water and begin to hurt as you peer to make out whatever lies in the shadow of a hedge or the dip of a pathway. Someone painting for pleasure might well decide to leave the shadows blank. More likely, though, he'll turn around, so that the sun warms his back and the shadows arrange themselves neatly out of sight behind each tree and bush. That's an acceptable view of things, yet the shadows will not have gone away, so he'll be painting only a part of the truth.

Shadows vanish only when light shines on them—light which may hurt and dazzle, light which can have nothing to do with darkness. Snow smothers, blurs and freezes while pretending to the purity of whiteness. But sunlight brings warmth to the muddy, secret places. It melts the snow, exposing what lies beneath, not in order to shame, but to bring cleansing and healing and new, vibrant life.

> ... *God is light and in him there is no darkness at all... if we walk in the light as he himself is in the light, we have fellowship with one another, and the blood of Jesus his Son cleanses us from all sin... If we confess our sins, he who is faithful and just will forgive us our sins and cleanse us from all unrighteousness.*

1 John 1:5, 7, 9

> ... *Christ loved the church and gave himself up for her, in order to make her holy by cleansing her with the washing of water by the word, so as to present the church to himself in splendour, without a spot or wrinkle or anything of the kind—yes, so that she may be holy and without blemish.*

Ephesians 5:25–27

Meditation

I wrote the passage which heads this chapter in order to work something through for myself with God. I was in the middle of researching a book on counselling. The Christian counsellor for whom I was writing chose, year in, year out, to shine God's light unwaveringly into dark places, even when he himself was attacked or misunderstood. I was finding out for the very first time about the extent of some terrible things which people can do to one another. After a while I found I didn't want to write about them—

I wanted to run away and hide. The night before one of my visits to interview the counsellor, it snowed. The next morning, as I drove through Wiltshire, the scene appeared just as I described it. God helped me to see where I was going wrong by reminding me of that strange image of white shadows time and time again, until I understood what he was saying to me.

It cost you so much, Lord, to shine your light right into our darkness. It costs you even more when we shield ourselves from that light, or when we choose to run back into the shadows. But once we consent to stay in your light, then you start a gentle bathing and restoring. The grime you found on the disciple's feet was as nothing to the filth each one of us carries, yet each day you come and cleanse our festering sores with infinite care—you, who should be waited on by angelic beings in heaven! Your special creams and ointments, unlike the ad-men's cons, over time begin to dispel our adolescent spottiness or our wrinkles of senile decay. And why? Because all along you see in us your bride. It's as though the prince comes riding by and recognizes his princess in the bag lady lying in the gutter. But this is no fairy-tale, no pantomime transformation scene. You keep tending to us. Over and over again you show us that your love is too great to let us return to squalor. Whatever it has—or will—cost, you will not give up on us, you will not rest, until you look on the face of your radiant bride!

See, I am black as night,
See, I am darkness: dark as hell.
Lord, thou more fair than light;
Heaven's sun the shadow: can suns dwell
With shades? 'twixt light and darkness what commerce?
True: thou art darkness, I thy Light: my ray
Thy mists and hellish fogs shall pierce.
With me, black soul, with me converse;
I make the foul December flowery May.
Turn thou thy night to me: I'll turn thy night to day.

From 'The Divine Lover'
by Phineas Fletcher (1582–1650)

St Peter once: 'Lord, dost thou wash my feet?'—
Much more I say: Lord, dost thou stand and knock
At my closed heart more rugged than a rock,
Bolted and barred, for thy soft touch unmeet,
Nor garnished nor in any wise made sweet?
Owls roost within and dancing satyrs mock.
Lord, I have heard the crowing of the cock
And have not wept: ah, Lord, thou knowest it.
Yet still I hear thee knocking, still I hear:
'Open to me, look on me eye to eye,
That I may wring thy heart and make it whole;
And teach thee love because I hold thee dear
And sup with thee in gladness soul with soul,
And sup with thee in glory by and by.'

'St Peter', by Christina Rossetti (1830–94)

UNCONDITIONAL LOVE

'But it's the sick who need a doctor!' he said. 'Yes, I know you have sick people in Europe and the States, but you also have hospitals here with all manner of drugs and laboratories, you have the latest complex machines to scan and probe. The staff think they're overworked—and they do work hard, but they stand some chance of achieving nearly all that's required. I'm talking about the sick with no hope. People who don't have a bed, in hospital or anywhere else—the ones who pick up parasites from sleeping in the gutter or from selling their bodies in order to feed their children.

'No, of course they don't have the money to pay me. I'm not in this for the money. Yes, I do know that it's hot and smelly and dangerous there and I'm aware that not everyone will respond with gratitude, that's not the point. No, I don't suppose many of them are very "civilized", though frankly I can do without some of the things which you think make up civilization. I'm sure they'll be a mixture of good and bad, like any other people the world over. I suspect that many will show a love and generosity which will astound me. You say they won't share my values? Maybe not, but if I live among them they'll see what my values are and whether they make sense or not—people learn when you model things.

'OK, it may go the other way. Someone may stab me in the back for what he thinks he can get out of me. I'm prepared for that too. Others will hate me because I'm trying to do something and they'll think I'm showing up their inadequacies. Whatever happens I know this won't be an easy job. If I wanted a comfortable life I'd set up a private clinic in Harley Street. The worst that can happen to me in a developing country like that is that I'll lose my life. But there again, had I been born there, like my patients, I'd expect to die young.

'You still don't understand why I'm going? They're human beings, aren't they? Human beings who are sick, most of them, who need a doctor. Yes, the need is ridiculously large but someone said it's better to light a candle than to curse the darkness. I'm choosing to light my candle away from the neon glow of ten thousand strip lights. Is that so very odd?'

> *... they said to his disciples, 'Why does he eat with tax collectors and sinners?' When Jesus heard this, he said to them, 'Those who are well have no need of a physician, but those who are sick; I have come to call not the righteous but sinners.'*

Mark 2:16–17

Meditation

Other religions have people reaching out to their god or gods through their own efforts. But God sent his Son to live and die in this world of his, a world which we had spoilt. He came and suffered here with us, the very people who had rebelled against him. He was determined to stay, even though we killed him. Then, instead of wiping out the world, Father God transmuted that death into something which issued in a new deal, a new covenant, a new beginning in his relationship with us.

No other gods took the path of embracing suffering in order to redeem humankind. We don't have to pull ourselves up by our own bootlaces. God offers his love to any who will receive it. The only condition is that we acknowledge our need of him. It's almost as though the worse we are, the more time and effort he puts into reaching out to us. Our not being good enough is no excuse as far as he is concerned—and so we have no place to hide from his love.

Indeed, rarely will anyone die for a righteous person—though perhaps
for a good person someone might actually dare to die. But God proves
his love for us in that while we still were sinners Christ died for us.

Romans 5:7–8

I'm not very good at showing unconditional love, Lord. I'm not prepared for the cost, the sacrifice. Love which is free to one can cost the other dear. When I see that kind of love in action, I find myself melting, tears in my eyes, because I know this is how things are meant to be. If I feel I have to do certain things to please someone, I can find myself resenting it and so react badly—but when someone shows me unconditional love, somehow it frees me to be a less selfish person. Help me to understand more of your unconditional love for me, for it's that love which turns my world, everyone's world, upside-down.

The spirit of the Lord God is upon me,
because the Lord has anointed me;
he has sent me to bring good news to the oppressed,
to bind up the broken hearted,
to proclaim liberty to the captives,
and release to the prisoners;
to proclaim the year of the Lord's favour...

Isaiah 61:1–2

Jesus, this was your ministry on earth. I am sick and my heart has been broken; please heal me. I'm in darkness; please shine your light. I'm oppressed; please cheer me. I'm hungry; please feed me. I'm in prison; please free me. All around I see others in a similar state and I cry out to you for them too. I think about a few by name now.

Dear Jesus, my wounded healer, please empower me with your love that knows no limits, and use me to reach out to these people, in your name. Amen.

The following is my favourite poem of all. I had to learn it by heart for English homework when I was about fourteen and it has come to mind many times since! It shows God being so gracious in serving and welcoming—but that's not all. He invites us to sit down and eat a feast which he sets before us! It's not a question of being rescued by the scruff of the neck. The tramp ends up as honoured guest; we're in for a good time!

Love bade me welcome: yet my soul drew back,
Guilty of dust and sin.
But quick-eyed Love, observing me grow slack
From my first entrance in,
Drew nearer to me, sweetly questioning
If I lacked anything.

'A guest,' I answered, 'worthy to be here.'
Love said, 'You shall be he.'
'I, the unkind, ungrateful? Ah my dear,
I cannot look on thee.'
Love took my hand, and smiling did reply,
'Who made the eyes but I?'

'Truth, Lord, but I have marred them; let my shame
Go where it doth deserve.'
'And know you not,' says Love, 'who bore the blame?'
'My dear, then I will serve.'
'You must sit down,' says Love, 'and taste my meat.'
So I did sit and eat.

'Love' by George Herbert
(1593–1633)

Since the Lord is in heaven I can only follow him by traces full of light and fragrance which he has left behind him. When I open the Gospels, I breathe the fragrance exhaled by the life of Jesus, and I know which way to run.

It is to the lowest that I hasten. I repeat with all confidence the humble prayer of the publican. Most of all I imitate the behaviour of Mary Magdalene, for her amazing—or, rather, loving—audacity, which delighted the heart of Jesus, has cast its spell upon mine.

It is not because I have been preserved from serious sin that I lift up my heart to God in trust and in love. I am certain that even if I had on my conscience every imaginable crime, I should lose nothing of my confidence, but would throw myself, my heart broken with sorrow, into the arms of my Saviour.

I remember his love for the prodigal son, I have heard his words to Mary Magdalene, to the woman taken in adultery. No—there is no one who could frighten me, for I know too well what to believe concerning his mercy and his love.

Thérèse of Lisieux (1873–97)

A COMPASSIONATE LOVE

By November the nights are long. Even at noon, the marshlands strike cold through the warmest of sheepskins. They won't let Alfric out, even by daylight, now that the floods have risen—and the floods won't subside until well after the spring melt, up high in the mountains.

The stump of his leg still pains him, though it was torn by the bear two springs ago and the infection has healed now. Still, he has to stay here, in the pole lodging, and help the women with the cooking—no work for a boy of fourteen summers! The women aren't unkind to him but he doesn't fit in. They laugh at his dreaming and tell him to skin the rabbit.

Hours later he finds a moment to pick up the hollow stem he's been working on. In the gloom of the pole lodging he tries to catch some light from the tallow, since the stem feels all wrong under his fingers. Yes, someone must have trodden on it—perhaps deliberately, since he left it tucked out of harm's way. The stem withstood the wind's battering as it grew out there on the marshland; it withstood the sun's bleaching too, but not this crushing underfoot. And who will fetch him another from the marshes now? This is the last from his small summer store and it had been showing his skill's increase. Yesterday it was shaping better than the others which he has worked and discarded, without daring to use them.

Swallowing his anger, Alfric prods the stem gently with his

finger, teasing it back into shape. Carefully, he binds a long piece of wispy grass around the crushed section, to give it strength. Then he wipes his blade on a leaf and peers again, wishing his fingers were neater and not so numb. Measuring by the length of his finger joints, he makes two cuts, three, then puts the pipe to his lips. He blows, gently, inaudibly at first, but soon with more confidence. Suddenly the gossip and laughter of the women fades to nothing. They leave their tasks and gather around him, staring.

A slow smile spreads over young Mari's face—it's almost as though she's seeing him for the first time. 'That's beautiful,' she whispers.

A far-away look softens old Idit's face, as nothing has since her man and child froze to death in that sudden snowstorm, too many winters ago to count.

Too crude as yet to be called music, the reedy notes float from the breath of Alfric's playing as the wind sighs over the marshes when the geese are calling—when they're beating, beating their wings, wild with longing for distant shores.

> *... a bruised reed he will not break,*
> *and a dimly burning wick he will not quench;*
> *he will faithfully bring forth justice.*

Isaiah 42:3

> *The Lord is near to the brokenhearted,*
> *and saves the crushed in spirit.*

Psalm 34:18

Meditation

Thank you, Lord, that even when I feel crushed and broken, you see the potential for music in me. Thank you that you invite all who are weary and heavy-laden to come to you. I fall into your arms now!

You have kept count of my tossings;
put my tears in your bottle.
Are they not in your record?

Psalm 56:8

In a night of pain I felt God say to me, 'I am willing to share in your pain, if you will let me.'

'But you're Lord of all! How can you want this? I don't want to give you pain!'

'You've given me your sin, so give me your pain, too. I love you so much that I'm willing to share both—and it will not destroy me.'

L.D.

I cannot tell how silently he suffered,
As with his peace he graced this place of tears,
Or how his heart upon the cross was broken,
The crown of pain to three and thirty years.
But this I know, he heals the broken-hearted,
And stays our sin, and calms our lurking fear,
And lifts the burden from the heavy laden,
For yet the Saviour, Saviour of the world, is here.

From 'I Cannot Tell',
by William Young Fullerton (1857–1932)

A LOVE FOR THOSE WHO SUFFER AND FEEL FAR FROM HIM

As a deer longs for flowing streams,
so my soul longs for you, O God.
My soul thirsts for God,
for the living God.
When shall I come and behold
the face of God?
My tears have been my food
day and night,
while people say to me continually,
'Where is your God?'

Psalm 42:1–3

And Love said, 'I hear your longing; it is like the wind sighing continually before my throne. I'm dry with your thirst, throat rasping, lips cracked, body heavy and crying out in desperation that it cannot live much longer. I'm wet with your tears, their hot saltiness courses down my skin too. I kept vigil through your cold hours when night merged into day and your sobs did not abate. I've felt your emptiness and exhaustion when day brings only more bleak hours of waiting. I know the time is long and that hope of any

89

improvement seems a bitter mockery to you. When I see those who pass by, spitting, "Where is your God?" I flinch, for I have heard those words before. But *you* do not say, "Where is your God?"—rather, "When shall I come and behold the face of God?" And I say to you, "Blessed are they that hunger and thirst after righteousness, for they shall be filled." And I say, "Blessed are those who are being purified in heart, for they shall see the face of God."'

These things I remember,
as I pour out my soul:
how I went with the throng,
and led them in procession to
the house of God,
with glad shouts and songs of thanksgiving,
a multitude keeping festival.

Psalm 42:4

And Love said, 'Others have poured libations of strong drink to the gods, but you pour out your soul to me. When your anguish, your anger flows through your words, your groans and tears, I receive them as your sacrifice, more precious than your praise in happier times. But the symphony of your life will not howl in a minor key for ever. Remember, when people mock, that those who know the fellowship of my sufferings will know also the unimaginable joy of my resurrection. As truly as I love, you will come again with glad shouts and thanksgiving, leading my people deeper in their rejoicing, because you have not only splashed about in my gentle streams but plunged under the thunder of my waterfalls. Know that, though all my waves swept over you, I have not—and never will—let you drown. And now, can you hear as the deep places in me call out to the deep places in you? Those who identify with my sufferings will experience to the full the unimaginable joy of my resurrection.'

Why are you cast down, O my soul,
and why are you disquieted within me?
Hope in God; for I shall again praise him,
my help and my God...

Psalm 42:5–6

Meditation

You might like to use this time to think about any you know who are experiencing something similar to the psalmist at the moment. Hold those people in God's presence. Ask him to speak words of comfort and reassurance to them—and be willing to let him do so through you.

If you find yourself in the same position as the psalmist, you might find it helpful to read his words of the psalm again and make them your own.

None other Lamb, none other Name,
None other Hope in heaven or earth or sea,
None other Hiding-place from guilt and shame,
None beside thee.

My faith burns low, my hope burns low,
Only my heart's desire cries out in me,
By the deep thunder of its want and woe
Cries out to thee.

Lord, thou art Life though I be dead,
Love's Fire thou art, however cold I be:
Nor heaven have I, nor place to lay my head,
Nor home, but thee.

'None Other Lamb', by
Christina Rossetti (1830–94)

If I stoop
Into a dark, tremendous sea of cloud,
It is but for a time; I press God's lamp
Close to my breast; its splendour, soon or late,
Will pierce the gloom: I shall emerge one day.

From 'Paracelsus', by Robert Browning
(1812–89)

ÄLL-KNOWING,
ÄLL-FILLING LOVE

Yachts flit like butterflies and canoes skim across the surface like
so many water boatmen. A battered coaster edges uncertainly from
the industrial area before chugging towards the open ocean. The
inlet shines, reflecting all the light from wide skies. One direction
stipples colours like an impressionist painting, the other gives the
pure cool wash of a water-colourist. I have to turn my head from
side to side to take in all this wide inlet, and even then some of its
low bays lie hidden from view. Birds crowd the one sandbank
which remains, tufting it like some crop ruffled by the wind. Other
flocks wheel like smoke in the distance, then rush into view and
after a splashing deceleration with legs splayed, they float,
squawking gently, preening. As the sun begins to lose its power
the land darkens, but the inlet shines on, its gentle luminosity lap-
ping in wavelets, soothing my tired eyes.

The night passes. By morning the ebbing tide has left acres of
drying mud here—what a difference a few hours makes! This place
smells still of salt and sea—a musty fishiness, green at the edges.
The mud's dark squelch fails to shine, except where trickling channels leak water towards the far-off ocean. Around the inlet's edge
the tide has deposited the night's detritus—old tyres and plastic
streamers picked over by scavengers—gulls masquerading in
white. Busy waders utilize every second, searching the mud for
worms and small crustaceans left behind by the ocean. Solitary

curlews probe deep with bills slender as curved skewers, while flocks of tiny sandpipers skitter to and fro, eyes on the surface. All will find rich pickings before the tide returns to cover their hunting ground, bringing fresh supplies and a chance to rest. It's coming now, as it does every day, unstoppable, covering beak-holes, clawprints and rubbish, pushing the birds back. Its force needs no haste as it edges to mingle with the trickle flowing down those drain-channels. It fills them, then, inexorably, creeping across the mud-flats. It searches out every depression, then every high place, until the last high corner of the last bay shines with an ocean of living water again.

> *O Lord, you have searched me and known me.*
> *You know when I sit down and when I rise up;*
> *you discern my thoughts from far away.*
> *You search out my path and my lying down,*
> *and are acquainted with all my ways...*
> *If I take the wings of the morning*
> *and settle at the farthest limits of the sea,*
> *even there your hand shall lead me,*
> *and your right hand shall hold me fast.*

Psalm 139:1–3, 9–10

Meditation

Lord, the water of your love floods right through me, searching out every corner of my life, of my being. You know me better than I know myself, Lord, and much better than anyone else. No human being, but only *you* will know me from before I was born until after I die. Only you are with me in the ebb and flow of each day, each year and decade. You see every little thing I do; you understand every thought that crosses my mind, from the affectionate and amusing to the stupid or despicable. Amazingly, despite your microscopic knowledge of the worst of me, you're determined to know me even more closely—not in order to shame or destroy but because you value me. Even if I let go of you it seems that, whatever happens, you keep holding on to me. The darkness, even my darkness, doesn't frighten you off. My sin's not a problem to you. You've dealt with that already.

Like a lover, you want to give me yourself. We're well past the honeymoon. Like a wife of many years, I know that, though my actions and thoughts may sometimes sadden, they never shock you. You won't get disillusioned, for you had no illusions in the first place. Instead, as inevitably as the tide floods the mud-flats, you keep searching me out, filling me with your transforming presence, so that, even in *my* life, boats can sail and birds can feed.

Help me to appreciate what you love about me, Lord, to understand the thought and care with which you put me together, even while I was in my mother's womb. You love me exactly as I am, and yet I'm only complete as you fill me. So, yes Lord, go on searching me with the waters of your love.

All outside is lone field, moon and such peace—
Flowing in, filling up as with a sea
Whereon comes Someone, walks fast on the white,
Jesus Christ's self...
To meet me, and calm all things back again.

Robert Browning (1812–89)

If I forget
Yet God remembers! If these hands of mine
Cease from their clinging, yet the hands divine
Hold me so firmly that I cannot fall;
And if sometimes I am too tired to call
For Him to help me, then He reads my prayer
Unspoken in my heart and lifts my care.

I dare not fear, since certainly I know
That I am in God's keeping, shielded so
From all else that would harm, and in the hour
Of stern temptation, strengthened by His power.
I tread no path in life to Him unknown;
I lift no burden, bear no pain alone.
My soul a calm, sure hiding place has found;
The everlasting arms my life surround.

'God, Thou Art Love',
by Robert Browning (1812–89)

THE CROWN

He's sitting there, holding up the crown, looking at it, turning it this way and that, examining the details. I've never thought highly of crowns, myself. Heavy, they weigh down human heads with too much power, too much expectation. Hard, cold and worth far too much, their flashy gems attract greed and fear and require the sacrifice of too many lives in the finding and the keeping. Yet the crown seems light in his hand. He's not gloating over it, like a miser with his gold, but seems to me more like a child, absorbed, full of wonder at a rainbow or a jewelled spider's web. The courtiers have gathered round to watch and he's sharing his delight with them.

The king laughs and turns to the craftsman on his left. 'If I wear this on my head,' he says, 'I can't see it. It may be my badge of office, my crowning glory, as it were, but it's not just when you're here that I take it off, hold it in my hand, look at it. I appreciate this new addition,' he points to an intricate corner which I'd not noticed. Tiny jewels form a pattern so delicate that I gasp. Even given the extraordinary quality of luminosity in this courtroom, how can those minute gems flash multi-coloured streamers of light clear across the chamber? And the way they are set and placed together—the skill of the craftsman reaches beyond anything I can imagine.

'What I'd like,' the king is saying, 'is something equally delicate to balance it.'

'A little filigree work perhaps, sire, set with emeralds, diamonds, and an opal in the centre?'

'Perfect. And while you're here, you see this part?' The king rubs at it gently with his finger.

The man on his right now leans forward, saying, 'Is it tarnished again, Father?' He holds out his hand for the crown, a hand pierced right through and stained red with blood.

I fear that its beauty will be smeared with the blood which seeps from the ugly wound. And then I understand. All the sacrifice comes from the king, from his son and from the craftsman. They were involved right from the forming of stones in extreme heat and pressure as carbon turned to diamond; they mined them in great toil and danger, guarded, kept and transported them. They cut and set the stones, heated, refined and shaped the gold. The skill, the creativity, the keeping clean—the cost is all theirs, their involvement in each stage complete. That is why the crown weighs light, why it can be borne aloft in great joy, be boasted of without grasping or shame; that is why it is so precious. Each atom of it is paid for fully. The gems are not hard and cold; they're warm and full of life. The whole crown lives and breathes praise to its maker and its owner. To him it is—we are—a glory and a delight in a way that no other crown was or ever can be, world without end.

You shall be a crown of beauty in the hand of the Lord,
and a royal diadem in the hand of your God.

Isaiah 62:3

Meditation

OK, Lord, there's a credibility gap here. No way do I feel like a flashy diamond, not even the tiniest fake ruby in some plastic toy crown. Right now I think a more appropriate image would be a muddy puddle. And I've met some real gems of your people, but even they're not flawless, so... why live in the land of make-believe?

What's that, Lord? Yes, I think I remember. That was a true story, wasn't it, in the papers some years ago? About a man whose house was always being burgled? He told his sons that after he died they would find their inheritance—something very precious, something they had seen every day in his house, but had never noticed. They looked and looked but never worked out what it could be until his will was read. The burglars never found it either, the huge diamond he'd had set into the flower design on the stained-glass window of his front door.

After their father died the sons examined the window in detail for the first time in their lives. They'd never really thought about it before; it was simply part of their lives as they were growing up—nice design, if you liked that kind of thing, well crafted. It might have been beautiful when new, but the grime of a thousand comings and goings had dulled it; dust stirred up by the lorries thundering outside had blurred its intricate corners.

They had been told that the gem lay in the centre of the rose and they peered at it now. Surely this dull glass had no more intrinsic value than an old milk bottle? Checking up on it would risk ruining the whole window. Yet why should their father lie? They decided to ask experts to take it out and clean it. Afterwards, valuers declared it to be worth the small fortune they had been promised.

So you're saying there's a gem hidden at the bottom of my muddy puddle, Lord? That I should take my eyes off my own inadequacies for a moment and think about you—that you made me, you continue to fashion me and, if sometimes you cut me with a hard edge, it's so that your light will flame out the better. And when life throws all its filth at me and I feel like mud, I must know that you have come to my aid before and will do so again. With the infinite care and skill of a craftsman you wipe away the layers of grime. Even when my own sin pollutes me from within, your very special cleansing agent, the holy blood of Jesus can penetrate, repair the cracks in me, make pure again. Help me to appreciate your love, to understand that you think I'm worth the trouble every time, to trust that you can and will do these things, yes, even for me!

I celebrate and shout because of my Lord God.
His saving power and justice are the very clothes I wear.
They are more beautiful
than the jewellery worn by a bride or a groom...
(He) will never be silent
till (we) are safe and secure, sparkling like a flame.

Isaiah 61:10; 62:1 (CEV)

Lord, what is man? Why should he cost thee
So dear? What had his ruin lost thee?
Lord, what is man, that thou hast over-bought
So much a thing of naught?
... What if my faithless soul and I
Would needs fall in
With guilt and sin?
What did the Lamb that he should die?
What did the Lamb that he should need,
When the Wolf sins, himself to bleed?
... Why should his unstained breast make good
My blushes with his own heart-blood?

O, my Saviour, make me see
How dearly thou hast paid for me...

From 'Charitas Nimia: or The Dear Bargain',
by Richard Crashaw (c. 1613–49)

You never enjoy the world aright till the sea itself floweth in your veins,
till you are clothed with the heavens and crowned with the stars, and
perceive yourself to be the sole heir of the whole world, and more than so
because men are in it who are every one sole heirs as well as you. Till you
can sing and rejoice and delight in God as misers do in gold and kings
in sceptres you never enjoy the world.

'First Century of Meditations' 29,
by Thomas Traherne (1637–74)

A LOVE THAT
VALUES US

He stuffed a couple more begging letters in the bin without opening them and felt a twinge of conscience. This had to be the best way, though. 'Compassion overload', wasn't that the phrase? He gave generously enough to a few charities which he knew and trusted. In the run-up to Christmas, though, letters from every conceivable good cause arrived daily, complete with heart-rending pictures of the starving—whether dogs, children or the aged. For goodness' sake, he was only human, he couldn't (and, in all fairness, shouldn't) give to them all.

Wearily he turned back to his computer. Little messages had appeared on the screen, announcing 'Disk full'. The wretched machine wouldn't save his current document. He'd have to delete some files before doing any more work.

The file manager churned up chunks of his past—the letters he'd written appealing for his son to get into the secondary school of his choice. What a battle that had been. Long over now, though! He pressed 'delete'.

Hey, those spreadsheets from the PTA accounts at his son's junior school; they dated from even farther back. How could he have forgotten all that counting of sticky coins from summer fêtes? The last one was only, what, four years ago? Life moved on so fast! His son didn't want him around school now—like most teenagers, he would do anything to avoid acknowledging the existence of embarrassing creatures called parents.

Current projects crowded most of the PC's disk space. These files had occupied most of his brain for the past few months. They used his skills as a bookkeeper and earned his living, but they too would become nothing but a disposable memory in a few years' time. Great chunks of life and work could be wiped from the PC's memory in a second! He shivered. Would his whole life be like that, flicked off at the switch of some cosmic computer, with all his actions erased as though they had never been? After he had sunk to the level of someone's brief pity, would he be chucked in the bin with the rest of the rubbish? Surely his life was worth more than that!

Are not five sparrows sold for two pennies? Yet not one of them is forgotten in God's sight. But even the hairs of your head are all counted. Do not be afraid; you are of more value than many sparrows.

Luke 12:6–7

Meditation

God of the universe, my capacity is limited, but yours is infinite. Help me to understand that you care about everything which concerns me—and so much more besides. I can't care for everything, but you can and do care, in enough detail to count the hairs on the head of every person who ever lived. When I feel overwhelmed by the needs of myself or others, help me to nestle closer to you.

... truly, one who touches you touches the apple of my eye.

Zechariah 2:8

Though I know that I don't earn your love, help me to understand that you treasure the good you see in me. You call your people the apple of your eye—which means that your instinct to watch over us is as sure as ours when it comes to guarding our own sight.

See, I have inscribed you on the palms of my hands...

Isaiah 49:16

Dear Jesus, my name might as well have been written on those nails that pierced your wrists, my rebellion helped drive them in. Instead, you engraved my name on the palms of your hands. It stays before you as a symbol of the new relationship you carved, after all hope had been corrupted and erased. I find that concept amazing. It shows that no way am I disposable so far as you are concerned. You won't edit out my name, my life, or my history with the flick of a switch. That would be impossible because I, and all who love you, have become part of you. You have identified your very self with each one of us. Only you are big enough to do that!

If, thinking of your frailty, you hold yourselves cheap, value yourselves by the price that was paid for you...

The Lord knows who are his own, like the farmer who sees the grain among the chaff. Don't be afraid that you will not be recognized, that storms will blow the grain under the chaff. The judge is not some countryman with a pitchfork, but the triune God. He is the God of Abraham, Isaac and Jacob, but he is your God too. You ask him for your reward and the giver himself is the gift. What more can you want?

'Be of Good Cheer', by St Augustine (384–430)

The work which His goodness began,
The arm of His strength will complete;
His promise is Yea and Amen,
And never was forfeited yet.
Things future, nor things that are now,
Nor all things below or above,
Can make Him His purpose forgo,
Or sever my soul from His love.

My name from the palms of his hands
Eternity will not erase;
Impressed on His heart it remains,
In marks of indelible grace.
Yes, I to the end shall endure,
As sure as the earnest* is given;
More happy, but not more secure,
The glorified spirits in heaven.

From 'A Debtor to Mercy Alone',
by Augustus Montague Toplady (1740–78)

* an earnest is money paid as an instalment to confirm a contract.

A LOVE THAT TAKES
PRIDE IN US

This piece was written by an infant school teacher:

'The moment I'd been dreading arrived. The final production of the Infant Nativity Play was the culmination of weeks of hard work and sleepless nights. Parents, friends and visitors packed the hall, sitting on hard chairs designed for six-year-olds. They seemed unconcerned about physical discomfort; the excited buzz of conversation and the looks on their faces showed they awaited the big event with eagerness.

'I stood in the wings as producer, looking on. As the play started I lived through every word and action. I saw nervous Alex stumble over words. Despite all my coaching, he still didn't know what to do with his hands. He stood in the wrong place, right in the way of the shepherds, then forgot to exit on time. Then I saw his parents, their faces aglow with pride and pleasure. Alex's eyes searched anxiously around the audience, before locking on to their look of approval. He gained confidence, relaxed—and even managed a smile.

'But I saw every fault in that performance magnified. I heard the king announce that his gift was 'Frank in Spence'. Mary dropped baby Jesus, one of the donkeys cried and refused to wear her mask and little Simon sang at record-breaking volume, one beat behind everyone else. After all my hard work I felt disappointed that the performance wasn't perfect. What would people think of such glaring flaws?

'But then I saw the sea of proud faces—the parents gazing proudly at their children. In their eyes their own child was a success, a star. After the play's final song the applause lasted for an exceptionally long time. Even after it ended, happy conversation crescendoed from the audience—the buzz at the beginning had been a faint whisper compared to the one at the end. As the parents left the hall I saw hardly a dry eye among them. The ones who spoke to me intimated that the latest multi-million West End hit couldn't have been more moving, more special. Any small mistakes had only added to the magic of the evening, they said, seeming surprised that I should mention this.

'And suddenly I saw that God looked on me in the same way— with pride and approval. Even my faults somehow added to my uniqueness—they were simply part of my growing up in him. After all, even Simon would learn to sing in time one day and clumsy Mary, in a year or two, would learn not to swing a 'baby' by one arm. As a producer, I'd wanted perfection and had been disappointed when things didn't work out that way—until I saw the effect that play had on both children and audience. God isn't some producer demanding endless, boring rehearsal of details to ensure that everything runs without a hitch. He never barks for perfection; he delights in me as I am.'

> *... I will write on you the name of my God, and the name of the city of my God, the new Jerusalem that comes down from my God out of heaven, and my own new name.*

Revelation 3:12

Meditation

So you really do want to be identified with me, Lord! I can't ignore your word, which says the same thing in so many places and in so many different ways. You *are* proud of all of us!

But you [all Christians] are a chosen race, a royal priesthood, a holy nation, God's own people, in order that you may proclaim the mighty acts of him who called you out of darkness into his marvellous light. Once you were not a people, but now you are God's people; once you had not received mercy, but now you have received mercy.

1 Peter 2:9–10

I can cope with the bit about having received mercy, but can't think why you'd choose me to proclaim your mighty acts, Lord. I don't feel in the least like a royal priest—that position sounds far too grand. And if your holy nation's the Church, I don't think many of us are really holy— certainly not me!

Yes, all right, I've seen nativity plays too. Christmas hasn't been the same since my children left primary school. I miss that feeling of overwhelming pride and surprise at what they can achieve. And yes, I've been moved to tears, seeing you in the kids with runny noses and the ones who sing out of tune. All right, I admit that they get your message across in a way which no one else could. Somehow they shine with your holiness, your glory, even though I know they're beating each other up backstage. Your words sound so strange at first, but perhaps they're beginning to make sense.

And because you are children, God has sent the Spirit of his Son into our hearts, crying, 'Abba! Father!' So you are no longer a slave but a child, and if a child then also an heir, through God.

Galatians 4:6–7

If you love and value me that much I will try to let these verses penetrate through my brain, to change my thinking. I'll let them go deep inside my heart. That would change the way I feel about myself and you, and change the way I react to others. But you'll have to help me, Lord. I'll only understand properly when your Spirit speaks to my spirit, when I *know* how you value me, and *accept* that you willingly identify with me—when you show me that all that you have is mine, because that's how much you love me, your child.

And the amazing thing is that, no matter how many children you adopt into your family, you love each as if he were the only one in the world, as if he were your first and best creation!

So in the centre of these thoughts of God,
Cyclones of power, consuming glory-fire,
As we fall o'erawed
Upon our faces, and are lifted higher
By his great gentleness, and carried nigher
Than unredeemèd angels, till we stand
Even in the hollow of his hand,—
Nay more! We lean upon his breast—
There, there we find a point of perfect rest
And glorious safety. There we see
His thoughts to us-ward, thoughts of peace
That stoop to tenderest love; that still increase
With increase of our need; that never change,
That never fail, or falter, or forget.
O pity infinite!
O royal mercy free!
O gentle climax of the depth and height
Of God's most precious thoughts, most wonderful, most strange!
'For I am poor and needy, yet
The Lord himself, Jehovah, thinketh upon me!'

From 'The Thoughts of God',
by Frances Ridley Havergal (1836–79)

His gifts and my possessions, both our treasures,
He mine, and I the ocean of His pleasures.
He was an ocean of delights from whom
The living springs and golden streams did come,
My bosom was an ocean into which
They all did run. And me they did enrich...
The king of glory in my soul did sit,
And to Himself in me He always gave
All that He delights to see me have.
For so my spirit was an endless sphere
Like God Himself, and heaven and earth was there.

From 'Silence', by Thomas Traherne
(1637–74)

A LOVE THAT
WEEPS AND LAUGHS

I take my paintbox and sit with it on my knee in the garden. The afternoon snoozes mellow as I prepare my palette and start mixing colours for the abstract I have in mind. First a pale green for the peace I feel, sitting here—the colour bleeds off into dusky pink edges of contentment. I breathe in the beauty of the soft air and my heart expands. I paint yellow for the warm, bright laughter which shines in from one corner, like the sun.

Something's spoiling the picture, though, a nagging worry. A black line zigzags across the paper. It makes me angry, so I add some splurges of livid red and immediately wish I hadn't. Regret's a fading bruise; its deep greyish purple creeps over my contentment. I had meant to be more positive.

I think about the people I love. One colour won't do; I need a shining rainbow, to express the differences. Overall, a rich blue sums up the way I feel—the only word I can think of is blessed to know them. But there again the ones you love can hurt the most. Memory lingers. I dull the royal blue with streaks of black, alternating stripes of thumping orange for sharp pain which tails off to the dull glow of a cigarette end. I can almost feel the smoke catching in my throat.

Others I love make me feel inferior. In the background I paint an uneasy nausea which threatens like a tidal wave, biding its time.

My life isn't all bad, though. I've given love sometimes without selfishness. A few people have said they value me, so I leave one corner as clear, white hope, praying I don't spill or spatter anything there. If I do, this corner will become like the rest, a mess of colours, of conflicting feelings, of good and bad. By the time I've added blobs of cerise for high excitement, a creeping brown for depression and lemon for pleasant surprise, the whole thing looks like a muddy puddle—the thing a small child might produce, given too much paint and no fresh paper!

But you, you feel anger, gentle affection, pain and forgiveness all at the same time. Undisputed victor, you sit serene in heavenly places, even as you fight the fierce war at the side of every one of your people, your heart churning within you. Lonely, yet complete in yourself, aching sadness and exuberant joy mingle without contradiction. You feel, you love, more deeply than any person could, yet those feelings never mar nor change your essence. How can I ever understand your paradoxes?

When real grief comes it smothers human laughter. My heart's paintbox has its limits. Its colours reflect light, subtracting, absorbing from the spectrum. My red traps the blue and yellow, imprisoning them. Put grey on top and even the red dims. You, on the other hand, paint with the light of your pure love. As we see its many colours, prism-split, the seeming contradictions of cyan, magenta and yellow focus and combine, spotlighting white again. Light paints movies, TV screens. Black remains your shadow, the nothingness where you are not.

Is it possible for me, like you, to paint a living picture, rather than this sodden, static mess? Will you show me what it is to feel your feelings more than my own, to paint not muddy abstractions but the light of the pure love that only you can fire within me?

... a God merciful and gracious,
slow to anger,
and abounding in steadfast love and faithfulness,
keeping steadfast love for the thousandth generation,
forgiving iniquity and transgression and sin,
yet by no means clearing the guilty...

Exodus 34:6–7

Meditation

Sometimes I wonder at God's wealth of feelings, which, unlike mine, seem to co-exist at one and the same time. His love makes him at once angry at the effects of sin and yet compassionate towards both sinner and victim. His heart must be filled with sadness at the terrible things which humans do, yet in Proverbs 8:31 we see him: 'rejoicing in his inhabited world and delighting in the human race'.

He is remote yet near. Isaiah 40:22 says: 'It is he who sits above the circle of the earth, and its inhabitants are like grasshoppers', yet Jesus was called Emmanuel, which means 'God is with us', and the Holy Spirit likes to live closer than my breath.

At once silent and holding a zillion conversations,
giving all your attention to a sparrow's ruffled feather
and shifting galaxies through space,
sitting at peace, in heavenly places
and travailing in the vomit and the filth,
incandescent with anger and billowing with mercy,
erupting with irrepressible joy and racked with unending grief,
melting with love, compassion, desire,
and all sufficient, set apart, holy...
I know a centime of what you feel, Lord.
I couldn't cope with more.
I may manage, with difficulty, one thing at a time,
but you feel all in a heartbeat and for eternity.
Help me remember that I am made in your image,
not you in mine.
Help me understand how you are at once
solemn and hilarious,
concerned and carefree,
fierce and gentle,
brim-full and empty with longing,
still and running faster than the wind.

Yet you are also harmony without discord,
light without shadow,
day without sleep,
dance without beginning,
love without end.
Divinity, I praise you!

Christine Leonard

And yet, God's emotions are so pure. Take laughter, for example.

When you laugh, Lord, it's not cruel or cynical,
you don't expose our weaknesses
to point up your own superiority,
you don't snip, snipe or satirise
at cardboard travesties of sex or race,
nor do you take someone who is trying to do a good job
and hoot at his big nose.
Yours is neither a polite titter
nor a snigger behind the hand in shame.
Untwisted, you never mean ill, or make dirty,
yet who else but you could have ordained
that we might reproduce in such sublime hilarity?

We laugh because we are embarrassed,
because we have put our foot in it
or fear looking ridiculous,
but your laughter, like the shared good jokes of family,
creates intimacy. It releases our tensions, our self-absorption;
it restores our balance and it soothes our pain.
Your laughter heals.

I think I hear yours as a belly laugh,
surfacing from wells of joy and celebration,
for though you know all about human frailty
and our ridiculous behaviour, also you see
goodness, endeavour, hope and love.
You are the father watching his toddler's energetic striving
to ascend the furniture or traverse the endless room,
who scoops her bruised ego in his proud arms,
and shares her whoops of delight as he whooshes her to the moon.

From the wholeness within yourself,
you touch with grace our absurd endeavours.
Your smile brings an end to our barrenness
with the undeserved promise of an Isaac.
And though your laughter is never divorced
from your compassion for the present aches of the world,
one day all will run as you intended,
with no more tears or darkness.
Love, joy and good, good laughter
will outlive them all.

'God's Laughter',
by Christine Leonard

A LOVE THAT SINGS

The warrior comes marching home. We have rushed to the walls and, while he is yet far off, we can see the sunlight glinting on his armour. We hear his shouts of triumph and are glad, because he has been fighting for us, he has won the victory for us.

His shout turns to a song, a triumphant song to the rhythm of his marching feet. At first whole phrases of it are blown away by the wind, but now we can hear clearly. His rich baritone lifts our hearts as nothing else in this world can. Our bellies vibrate to the deep notes. Suddenly the day seems bright and full of energy. Even the stones in front of him seem to shake, to come alive, to sing with him.

His wife and child are running out to greet him now. He hands his spear to a foot soldier, embraces his wife and sweeps the little one up into his arms. They are laughing and joining in his song, the soprano blending in harmony, clear but soft, the child's descant squeaking precariously, but with such joy that she sounds like the sweetest wren.

Though all the soldiers and townspeople have joined in the song now, the warrior's voice at the centre sets the tune, the rhythm; his voice remains the strongest and best. Unlike the warrior-kings of neighbouring towns he sings, not of his great battle and victories, but of his joy in coming home and of his great love for each one of us in the town. In times of peace this, our king, leads us—but as a servant, not a dictator. He rules us with humility and love.

He sings now to the servants, to the traders and to the young bloods. He sings to the craftsmen and the farmers, to the old and the babies, to the sick and the busy—and he sings to me. His words mean something different to each individual, for he knows each well—but the music carries his love for us far deeper into our beings than words alone could do. Somehow this extraordinary song is opening us up to the hugeness of his delight and pride and exultation, not over his victory but in us. The notes surge through us, resonating deep within our bodies, souls and spirits, filling each of us with something of his strength. The tired, the weak, the infirm feel ready for anything now, because he believes in them, he loves them. He makes them an especial gift of his strength and his joy.

The Lord, your God, is in your midst,
a warrior who gives victory;
he will rejoice over you with gladness,
he will renew you in his love;
he will exult over you with loud singing,
as on a day of festival.

Zephaniah 3:17–18 (RSV)

Meditation

We sing praises to God. As people who love him always have, right from the beginning of the Bible. How else should we worship one so amazing, so divine, than with words whose poetry distils meaning, with notes whose harmonies express the way our hearts unite to fear his name, and with music whose rhythms throb out our deepest longings and passion? In singing we lose our inhibitions and can express our happiness, our pain, our love. As we sing together we harmonize and become one; something shifts and the world takes on a different shape.

But can it be true that God sings, exults, rejoices over us? Imagine it: Father, Son and Holy Spirit singing over us together, with the angels joining in!

Lord, I've never heard you singing, not properly, though I've caught a note or two sometimes in a church full of worship, on a windswept beach or at dawn in a spring wood. I find it hard to imagine the sounds of heaven, I'm dumbfounded that you find anything to sing about in me, but you say that you do. You're God; it's not for me to doubt you. If you sent your Son to die for me, if I am worth that much in your eyes, then to you I suppose I must be worth the singing. Help me to take it in, to remember, to ponder in my heart that you, the Almighty, sing, rejoice and exult over me!

By day the Lord commands his steadfast love,
and at night his song is with me,
a prayer to the God of my life.

Psalm 42:8

What song have you been singing to me these past nights, Lord? A tender lullaby? Something to stir, envision, give me hope? A haunting love song, full of sadness and longing? Something more full of joy and energy than an Irish jig? Help me to feel the rhythm of your song to me tonight, to sense its mood and hear its harmony. May your song be with me even as I sleep, bathing me with all that is good and pure and lovely.

Bright is the ring of words
When the right man rings them,
Fair the fall of songs
When the singer sings them.
Still they are carolled and said—
On wings they are carried—
After the singer is dead
And the maker buried.

From 'Songs of Travel' XIV,
by Robert Louis Stevenson (1850–94)

Such music (as 'tis said)
Before was never made,
But when of old the sons of morning sung,
While the Creator great
His constellations set,
And the well-balanced world on hinges hung,
And cast the dark foundations deep,
And bid the weltering waves their oozy channel keep...

For if such holy song
Enwrap our fancy long,
Time will run back and fetch the age of gold,
And speckled Vanity
Will sicken soon, and die,
And leprous Sin will melt from earthly mould,
And Hell itself will pass away,
And leave her dolorous mansions to the peering day.

From 'Hymn on the Morning of
Christ's Nativity',
by John Milton (1608–74)

118

A GENEROUS LOVE

Farhorn stepped into the glade. At last he had found it. The trees, rustling a pale silver-green, seemed to part their narrow leaves to let him in. A path, barely worn, took him straight to the tree, the tree in the middle of the wood—the middle of the world, some said.

His hooves made no sound on the soft carpet of grass and moss. Under the wood's thick canopy the light was dim, but the tree at the centre shone gold. Its brightness came from within and reflected from one leaf to another. They shifted in the breeze, like a many-faceted gold necklace or a suit of chain-mail. Farhorn thought that he had never seen anything so beautiful and it was with a sense of awe that he approached the tree.

'Come, come and drink!' Did a deep voice speak the words or did he merely hear them inside his head? It did not seem to matter. He noticed it now—a stream emerging from the darkness of the wood and broadening into a still pool beneath the golden tree. Could he really drink from that pool?

'Come, come and drink!' His hooves sank deeper into a damp carpet of moss as he approached. As he bent his head he could see gold leaves reflected in the water and above them the blue sky.

He hesitated for a moment, partly because he did not want to disturb the reflections and partly because, faced with that water, he did not feel good enough. But there again, the words had a tone of gentle command as well as invitation. He opened his mouth and found himself swallowing gulps of the sweetest, cleanest water which he had ever tasted. Cool, but not too cold, it seemed to contain at once the sherbet fountain of youth and the maturity of red wine which had been ageing long years in oak casks, hidden deep in forgotten cellars. As Farhorn drank he felt that he was taking in the goodness of rich milk, the vitamins of carrot juice, the dizzy intoxication of champagne. It soothed his weariness and woke him up again. He felt like a young foal, felt he could do anything. And yet his muscles, which had been taut with the effort of his epic journey here, relaxed and he could equally happily have lain down and slept for centuries.

He felt a deep wisdom dawning within him, a sense that he had grown up, had begun to understand. Exactly what it was he understood he had no idea. He could not have put it into words, except that a hope grew inside him. A hope that he would no more have to struggle on alone, up hills, over rocks, through thorny undergrowth or raging torrents, past men or beasts who would love to trap, maim, or kill him. Now he had drunk from the pool at the centre of the world, even if he did have to face these things, it would be all right. He would complete his errand, he would deliver the Message. Even if he failed, it would still be all right!

An energy surged within him and he felt a great neigh rise up from his belly. He could see the path which led out to the other side of the wood. Beyond that lay the great mountain range of the Western Klonders and beyond that again the Great Desert with its fierce nomadic tribes and its ascetic wizards, who posed perhaps the greatest danger of all. But Farhorn felt such power in his muscles that he set off at a trot, which turned into the most joyful of gallops as he emerged from the other side of the little wood, on to the grassy plain.

So I tell you to ask and you will receive, search and you will find, knock and the door will be opened for you... As bad as you are, you still know how to give good gifts to your children. But your heavenly Father is even more ready to give the Holy Spirit to anyone who asks.

Luke 11:9, 13 (CEV)

Meditation

Your gifts are so good, Lord. It's not that you always give me health or wealth, but you do give me all that I need, in easy circumstances and in difficult ones.

Thank you that the Bible speaks in such concrete terms of your extravagant generosity, which is rooted in your love for us. Most amazing of all, you give me yourself: help me to dare to drink deeply of you.

... give, and it will be given to you. A good measure, pressed down, shaken together, running over, will be put into your lap...

Luke 6:38

I would feed you with the finest of the wheat, and with honey from the rock I would satisfy you.

Psalm 81:16

Lord, I've been exhausted in a rocky desert, and you've fed me with honey. When you provide a banquet, it's likely to be in the presence of my enemies. You love me enough not to spoil me like some year-round Father Christmas, but you know exactly when I need a surprise gift with that millionaire touch about it. Then I know that it comes from you and that you're still in control.

He brought me to the banqueting house, and his banner over me was love.

Song of Solomon 2:4 (RSV)

Perhaps it takes someone who has almost nothing, materially, to appreciate God's generosity to the full. Afua Kuma, a simple farmer and traditional midwife from Ghana, could not read or write, but her praises of Jesus in the Twi language were recorded on tape and then translated into a booklet. Whenever I read her words, I too want to praise him for all that he gives us.

> When you ask something from Jesus,
> he doesn't place it into your hands,
> but when you return to your room, it is there—
> if he had given it you, you couldn't have carried it!...
> He is the great Grass Hut, the Shed which shelters mice,
> the 'Thump! Thump!' of the pestle,
> he beats down our hunger.
> Hard-wood hoe-handle, which brings us our food.
> Onyankopɔn Amponyinam: God the provider,
> who has medicine for our hunger.
> Ɔerekyi Sakyi: the Elephant Hunter,
> whose family's cooking pots
> have no place for little mushrooms...
> Pencil of teachers
> which brings knowledge to the children! ...
> Jesus is the day of month when I get my pay.
> The Chief of Christians
> whose shade tree grows money...
> the big House which takes in travellers.
> The unused farm where grows the wild yam.
> The Sea, which gives us fat fish.
> The first-born Child who knows Death's antidote.
> Jesus is the wall which bars death from entry,
> and makes many hearts leap for joy.

From *Jesus of the Deep Forest*
by Afua Kuma

God's hands are round, and smooth, that gifts may fall
Freely from them, and hold none back at all.

'God's Hands', by Robert Herrick
(1591–1674)

God gives not only corn, for need,
But likewise sup'rabundant seed;
Bread for our service, bread for shew;
Meat for our meals, and fragments too:
He gives not poorly, taking some
Between the finger, and the thumb;
But, for our glut, and for our store,
Fine flour press'd down, and running o'er.

'To God', by Robert Herrick
(1591–1674)

He is a path if any be misled;
He is a robe, if any naked be;
If any chance to hunger, he is bread;
If any be a bondman, he is free;
If any be but weak, how strong is he!
To dead men life he is, to sick men health;
To blind men sight, and to the needy wealth;
A pleasure without loss, a treasure without stealth.

From 'He Was Made Man',
by Giles Fletcher (1588–1623)

As thou art all, so be thou all to me,
First, midst and last, converted, one and three;
My faith, my hope, my love; and in this state
My judge, my witness, and my advocate.

From 'To Heaven', by Ben Jonson
(1573–1637)

INESCAPABLE LOVE

I looked after him from the moment he was born. As a boy he'd tell me everything and we'd explore the world hand in hand. His discoveries would be my discoveries and when he trapped his finger in the door my own throbbed for days.

We played hide-and-seek often in the forest and he learned well the skills of silent stalking. But as a boy he wanted to be found—if not immediately then before nightfall. There would be laughter in the finding—and mugs of hot chocolate before bedtime.

As he grew up, his skulking hardened into something that was neither sport nor game. All of a sudden he acted like one hunted and it was from my presence that he fled—I, who had never given him any cause for fear and who had protected him with my life through the years when he could do nothing for himself.

He ran off into the city and lost himself on the fairground rides, making it clear that to swoop and dive with me by his side would tame the thrill. From a discreet distance I kept my eye on him. Among all those people, all that movement, I could pick him out—even in the maze of distorting mirrors, or the tacky 'House of Horror'. I couldn't prevent him from losing himself, though, among the pleasures and the pressures. His affection, so freely given as a child, narrowed as he shut down, restricting himself to making demands on friends and lovers. Sometimes he gave a little love to them and seemed to grow an inch or two, but more often he shrank away, becoming wizened and bitter, even in his youth.

Later, when he found some control, some success, other people thought he was growing up. Then work took more and more of his time and attention. Soon he had nothing left for himself, or his friends, let alone me. That's been the situation for some years now. He's convinced that he has everything worked out, that he's built a fortress strong enough to hide him for ever, so that he need give nothing away. He didn't stop to think that I am not one to smash down walls. My love has the strength and constancy of breathing, not of a battering ram. It reaches him through memories and dreams, against which he has no more defence than he does against the air itself.

Sometimes I see an unexpected kindness catch him off guard, piercing the cold metal of his armour like a tiny, red-hot needle. These brief moments act merely as pinprick irritations, but my prayers reach farther than an arm can throw or a gun can shoot. I have seen the person he is and my love for that person will never die. I know that he will find me again. At least, he will think that it is he who has found me! On that day he will know that he is arriving at a safe resting-place after his long journey—and I will run to meet him.

> *Where can I go from your spirit?*
> *Or where can I flee from your presence?*
> *If I ascend to heaven, you are there;*
> *if I make my bed in Sheol, you are there.*
> *If I take the wings of the morning*
> *and settle at the farthest limits of the sea,*
> *even there your hand shall lead me,*
> *and your right hand shall hold me fast.*
> *If I say, 'Surely the darkness shall cover me,*
> *and the light around me become night,'*
> *even the darkness is not dark to you;*
> *the night is as bright as the day,*
> *for darkness is as light to you.*

Psalm 139:7–12

Meditation

You don't force yourself on me, Lord, yet you don't give up on me either, even when I keep running from you, spitting angry abuse in your face. Like the father in the story of the lost son, or the shepherd looking for the lost sheep, you look out for me every day, however far I wander away from you. You love your children, in spite of everything, and your love is the strongest force in the universe!

If you weren't pure love, who could stand before your awesome presence? Help me not to fear but to welcome your relentless pursuit of me, help me to rest secure in your inescapable love.

The poem which follows tells of one rebelling against his God. 'Board', in this case, means 'altar'—a shocking image, since to strike it, in the seventeenth century, was tantamount to blasphemy.

I struck the board, and cry'd, No more.
I will abroad.
What? Shall I ever sigh and pine?
My lines and life are free; free as the road,
Loose as the wind, as large as store...
Away; take heed:
I will abroad...
But as I rav'd and grew more fierce and wild
At every word,
Me thought I heard one calling, Child;
And I replied, My Lord.

From 'The Collar', by George Herbert
(1593–1633)

Who will separate us from the love of Christ? Will hardship, or distress, or persecution, or famine, or nakedness, or peril, or sword? ... No, in all these things we are more than conquerors through him who loved us. For I am convinced that neither death, nor life, nor angels, nor rulers, nor things present, nor things to come, nor powers, nor height, nor depth, nor anything else in all creation, will be able to separate us from the love of God in Christ Jesus our Lord.

Romans 8:35, 37–39

Jesus said to me, 'My grace in you is like the sun. Sometimes the sun shines brightly so that everyone can see it, at other times it is hidden behind a cloud; although you cannot see it, the brightness is still there. In the same way my grace is always with you.'

'Grace', by Margery Kempe (1373–?)

Tennyson's most famous poem tells how his faith wavered in the face of the loss of a very dear friend.

If e'er when faith had fall'n asleep,
I heard a voice 'believe no more'
And heard an ever-breaking shore
That tumbled in the Godless deep;

A warmth within the breast would melt
The freezing reason's colder part
And like a man in wrath the heart
Stood up and answered 'I have felt.'

No, like a child in doubt and fear:
But that blind clamour made me wise;
Then was I as a child that cries,
But, crying, knows his father near;

And what I am beheld again
What is, and no man understands;
And out of darkness came the hands
That reach through nature, moulding men…

Love is and was my King and Lord,
And will be, though as yet I keep
Within his court on earth, and sleep
Encompassed by his faithful guard,

And hear at times a sentinel
Who moves about from place to place,
And whispers in the world of space,
In the deep night, that all is well.

From 'In Memoriam' CXXIII and CXXV,
by Alfred, Lord Tennyson (1809–92)

A LOVE THAT'S NEW EVERY MORNING

He felt as though he had lain awake most of the night. Anxious thoughts fluttered fears that echoed hollow in his stomach—and, once again, he couldn't stop them. The stuffy summer night had made him sweat and he'd thrown off the bed covers. Shivering now, he pulled them round him again, finding in them a kind of security. Still he had no idea what he could do about the source of his worries. He wasn't used to feeling this alone—nor to having too much time and nothing worth doing with it. He hadn't so much lost a job and a wife, as lost himself.

He blinked. The short night had ended and sunshine streamed through the thin curtains. He must have dozed a few times without realizing it. His muscles ached, his mouth tasted of sour metal and he longed for the oblivion of deep sleep. From past experience, though, he knew he was unlikely to drop off again. He got up, slow and unusually stiff.

A hot cup of tea cleared his head a little, and in the shower he started to relax as the warm water scudded through his hair, massaging his scalp and sending the acrid sweats of the night spiralling down the drain. He dried himself on the thick, rough towel. The damp air relaxed the grip of the asthmatic tightness which kept binding his chest these days. He flung on a tracksuit and found himself in the garden almost before thinking about it.

Everything was so quiet. No car moved yet along the street; no children (or parents) yelled, no dogs yapped. Even the planes were absent, but he heard a bee bumbling its way about and felt the collision when it bumped into a stem of golden rod, shaking a shower of dew which landed on the thick fur of its bottom. It struck him as funny and he found himself chuckling, quietly, so as not to wake the neighbours. He thought of all the mornings like this which he had wasted, either in bed or rushing off on some plane to another city, another skyscraper.

Through the cool air, already the sun warmed his skin. He took deep breaths, filling lungs accustomed to diesel fumes from the monster lorries which panted just over the fence all day long. Now he smelt damp grass and roses. A robin flew down on to the old tree stump where sometimes his wife had scattered crumbs. The old tightness began to return when he realized afresh that she wouldn't be doing that any more. But the bird was looking at him with intelligent eyes.

'I haven't had breakfast yet either!' he told it, out loud, yet he didn't feel hungry. Instead suddenly he had the urge to do something mad, like run round the garden at top speed. He wished he'd kept Ellie's swing; he would have stood on it and soared high—higher than the robin as it flew off, over the fence.

I could plant some vegetables, he thought. I'll buy the seeds today. He remembered once—years ago, in a friend's garden—eating tomatoes, red and warm from the sun. He found a pencil and pad of paper in the house. Ideas were coming so fast he had to write them down or risk losing them for ever—and some of them might just work to jolt him from the heaviness of his grief. Yes, one or two might well work!

> *The steadfast love of the Lord never ceases,*
> *his mercies never come to an end;*
> *they are new every morning;*
> *great is your faithfulness,*
> *'The Lord is my portion,' says my soul,*
> *'therefore will I hope in him.'*

Lamentations 3:22–24

Meditation

Thank you, Lord, that each night acts as a full stop; that we can begin each new day with a new sentence, a new paragraph, a change of thought, of mood. Though you have lived for ever, you are never exhausted, never uncreative. You are the God of new beginnings, who invented snowdrops and grandchildren; the God who, all through history, has taken fallen people and given them a fresh start. Supremely, you are the God of resurrection. Like the breeze on reaching the summit of a gruelling hill on a humid afternoon, your presence refreshes me. You lift my heaviness more surely than breathing the air after a summer thunderstorm or the smell of bacon in a clean, yellow kitchen. Your love, your belief in me, your practical concern, all bring real hope of a new start—and when you free me from the prisons I make for myself, you heap no recriminations; my past is cleaned, my future full of possibilities.

Like sunshine, a morning of promises appears.
Shining, exploring even the darkest tunnels, filtering through barriers.
Like a never-ending stream pouring over thirsty ground,
stretching across far horizons.
Opening a new rosebud with just a touch.
Gently lighting up the dew on a fragile spider's web.
Warm, breaking through the clouds on a winter's day,
reaching everyone.

'God's Love', by Janine Madge

When Mary thro' the garden went
There was no sound of any bird,
And yet, because the night was spent,
The little grasses lightly stirred,
The flowers awoke, the lilies heard.

When Mary thro' the garden went,
The dew lay still on flower and grass,
The waving palms about her sent
Their fragrance out as she did pass,
No light upon the branches was.

When Mary thro' the garden went,
Her eyes, for weeping long, were dim,
The grass beneath her footsteps bent,
The solemn lilies, white and slim,
These also stood and wept for him.

When Mary thro' the garden went,
She sought, within the garden ground,
One for whom her heart was rent,
One who for her sake was bound,
One who sought and she was found.

'When Mary Thro' the Garden Went',
by Mary Coleridge (1861–1907)

… Generations have trod, have trod, have trod;
And all is seared with trade; bleared, smeared with toil;
And wears man's smudge and shares man's smell: the soil
Is bare now, nor can foot feel, being shod.
And for all this, nature is never spent;
There lives the dearest freshness deep down things;
And though the last lights off the black West went
Oh, morning, at the brown brink eastward, springs—
Because the Holy Ghost over the bent
World broods with warm breast and with ah! bright wings.

From 'God's Grandeur',
by Gerard Manley Hopkins (1844–89)

EVERLASTING LOVE

She crawled out from under the bushes. She had heard his voice calling to her for some time. Finally he had crouched down, so that his head was on a level with hers and held out his hand. She had cowered behind the brambles, frightened because he had searched her out, mortified that he had found her. He had spoken gently but she couldn't understand much of what he was saying. Finally, through the thorny branches she had looked into his eyes, wondering how they could smile a clear welcome and register so much concern at the same time. It was his eyes that held her and made her feel safe. She knew she was taking a risk in acting on her impression that he had come to help, not harm her.

The branches scratched her skin as she wriggled her way out of the shelter which she had made. She clamped her hands over the sore places, curling in on herself, avoiding the hand he held out to her. Still, on this open road she must rely on him for protection. She followed at his heels, like a dog. He kept turning to speak to her, motioning her to walk beside and not behind him, offering her his arm for support, as though she were a lady and he a real gent. At length she relented and couldn't help relaxing a little as she felt the warmth of his large hand cover the skinny coldness of hers. When she tripped on a tree root she clung tight and his strength saved her from falling.

As they walked along he said very little, yet this was not an awkward silence. He seemed to appreciate that she was unused to company. For her, conversation was like reading to a child who had never been to school—a skill which would take time and patience to acquire.

She noticed things, though. She noticed that the man knew where he was going. Even when the track forked in several directions, he never hesitated. Her confidence in him grew. Once she heard the angry sound of an animal and froze, clutching tight at his hand. He smiled and pointed to a squirrel-like creature, chattering and hissing like a miniature wildcat in the tree. He stopped sometimes and picked fruit or wild mushrooms to eat. She knew from her own experiments in living off the land how much tasted foul or made her stomach ache—yet everything he offered her tasted good, so good! She began to enjoy a new-found energy, where she had known only the weakness of hunger—and felt that she could walk along the road with this man for ever.

She wanted to ask him so many questions and had even begun to form the words in her head when she realized that she no longer held his hand. He had disappeared! She looked this way and that, trying not to panic. They had been walking for a couple of hours and she had no idea of her whereabouts in this great forest. Then she heard a noise—something huge was crashing through the undergrowth, coming towards her. Without thinking she dived for cover and found her feet sinking in a bog which lay to the side of the track. The more she struggled to free one foot, the more the other sank. Cold, peaty mud was creeping up above her knees now, trapping her.

She no longer cared about the beast, whatever it was. 'Help!' she shouted. 'Help me!' The man who had seemed so kind, so strong, why had he disappeared, just when she needed him most? The cold mud oozed over her stomach; she was sinking faster than ever. Why had she let him slip off like that? Why had she not held on to him more tightly? Up to her chin now, she had time only for one last yell—but she was going down fighting.

Her nose, her eyes were covered. Desperate, unable to draw breath, she waved her arms above her head. Suddenly she felt someone grasp her hands and start to pull her out. It took a while, but she knew she would be all right. Her relief felt even stronger than the terror had done. Afterwards he wrapped her in warm cloth to stop her shivering and wiped her eyes with something soft. Only then did she see the bear lying dead and enormous at her feet.

'I thought you'd gone!' she said, reaching for the man's hand—which was when she noticed the claw marks down his arm. 'I let go of you.'

'I take no one's hand unless they are willing,' he said. 'But those who choose to walk with me come to learn that, though sometimes they lose their grip, I don't abandon them, not when it matters.'

He took a clean, dry blanket from his pack, wrapped it around her and led her to a sheltered place at the foot of a great tree. There he cradled her head on his lap. 'You are weary, child,' he said. 'Sleep now!'

> *The eternal God is your refuge, and underneath are the*
> *everlasting arms; he will thrust out the enemy from before you,*
> *and will say, 'Destroy!'*

Deuteronomy 33:27 (NKJ)

Meditation

Your arms are strong enough, Lord, to stretch out across the universe and catch me, even though I might be free-falling through never-ending space. Let me curl up now, safe in the palm of your hand.

> *… I have loved you with an everlasting love;*
> *therefore I have continued my faithfulness to you.*

Jeremiah 31:3

Thank you, Lord, that love undergirds everything, that it reaches everywhere and lasts beyond all time.

God be with thee in every pass,
Jesus be with thee on every hill,
Spirit be with thee on every stream,
Headland and ridge and lawn;

Each sea and land, each moor and meadow,
Each lying down, each rising up,
In the trough of the waves, on the crest of the billows,
Each step of the journey thou goest.

'The Pilgrims' Abiding',
Traditional Celtic

RIVERS OF LOVE

I've been sitting here on the dry grass for hours now. It's too hot, really. I should move into the shade, but the woods are a long way from the river and somehow I can't stop watching everyone. Young children, held by the hand, paddle at the edge where the bank's not too steep. Some splash, whooping with delight, while others, with faces intent, watch the tiny fish as they dart from the shelter of the weed. Some adults stay at the edge too, sitting on the bank, swishing their feet gently through the water, gazing dreamily up at the blue, blue sky. Others wade knee deep, trousers rolled up, or skirts held high, taking care to keep out of the way of the splashing children.

A small girl is learning to swim. She seems safe; the current's not too strong there. Further out they're simply whizzing by, the swimmers and those on inflatable lilos. That's what scares me. I've seen a few trying to battle against the current, but in the end they tire of travelling backwards and go with the flow, like everyone else. And then they disappear out of view. Do they know something that I don't? Maybe the current will land them on the bank somewhere downstream, so that they can hike back here through the fields. That wouldn't be too comfortable, with bare feet!

It's hard to identify individuals shooting past, nine-tenths submerged, with their hair styled by the water. I can't be sure that I've seen a single one of them coming back. Suppose there's some great weir or waterfall around the corner, which batters them to death? But surely there would be notices here, and lifeguards and a barrier to stop people going out too far? Suppose they keep floating down-river until night falls and then succumb to exposure as the temperature drops?

Yet they all look so happy—maybe it's foolish to sit here all by myself! Maybe I should at least dip my toe in the water; I'm so very hot and thirsty. And if I find it's the right temperature, I could paddle a little. Of course, I can't swim. I never learned, mainly because I never dared take my feet off the bottom. My mother told me I was daft, that if the water held everyone else up, of course it would hold me. But I couldn't bring myself to believe her. That four-year-old, though, she's doing really well. It puts me to shame. Maybe if I stayed within my depth, so that I could save myself with my foot on the bottom...?

Yet it's odd, but the ones I envy, the ones who are having the best time, are those far out, rocketing by, completely out of control, so far as I can see. They let the river carry them where it will. They seem so full of fun, living dangerously—and living to the full. They know where they're going, too—to wherever the river goes—to the sea, perhaps, to the ocean. Unless I join them, I guess I'll never know.

The man took me back to the temple, where I saw a stream flowing from under the entrance... The man walked east... five hundred metres downstream. He told me to wade through the stream there, and the water came up to my ankles. Then he measured another five hundred metres downstream and told me to wade through it there. The water came up to my knees. Another five hundred metres downstream the water came up to my waist. Another five hundred metres downstream, the stream had become a river that could be crossed only by swimming... We walked to the river bank, where I saw dozens of trees on each side. The man said: 'This water flows eastwards to the valley of the River Jordan and empties into the Dead Sea, where it turns the salt water into fresh water. Wherever this water flows, there will be all kinds of animals and fish, because it will bring life and fresh water to the Dead Sea. From En-Gedi to Eneglaim, people will fish in the sea and dry their nets along the coast. There will be as many kinds of fish in the Dead Sea as there are in the Mediterranean Sea.

Ezekiel 47:1–10 (CEV)

Meditation

Do I dare to see myself paddling, then bathing in God's river? Will it take me somewhere I don't want to go? Will it destroy me? What *am* I saying; how could God's love destroy me? If it can bring life even to the Dead Sea, where nothing lives, perhaps it can bring a newness of life to me!

But if it doesn't drown, will it dry up on me? Psalm 1 says that God's people are 'like trees planted by streams of water which yield their fruit in season and their leaves do not wither'. So do I dare plunge into that river, take my feet off the bottom and entrust my little life to the great flow of God's love? It's what I want, but you know I'm scared, so help me, Lord!

How precious is your steadfast love, O God!
All people may take refuge in the shadow of your wings.
They feast on the abundance of your house,
and you give them drink from the river of your delights.

Psalm 36:7–8

O the deep, deep love of Jesus,
Vast, unmeasured, boundless, free!
Rolling as a mighty ocean
In its fullness over me.
Underneath me, all around me,
Is the current of thy love;
Leading onward, leading homeward,
To my glorious rest above.

From 'O the Deep, Deep Love of Jesus',
by S. Trevor Francis (1834–1925)

O Love that wilt not let me go,
I rest my weary soul in thee;
I give thee back the life I owe,
That in thine ocean depths its flow
May richer, fuller be.

From 'O Love that Wilt Not Let Me Go',
by George Matheson (1842–1906)

OCEANS OF LOVE

They're clumsy and embarrassing on land, but I relish the freedom that flippers give me in the water. With a flick of my foot I can shoot sideways, up or down at will, or with a little effort speed forward almost like a dolphin, or so I like to think! Best of all I love to lie lazily floating face down on the surface, breathing through my snorkel tube. The warm Mediterranean waters lap around my body, supporting it horizontally with no effort on my part. I have found that I can lift rocks, or even people—they weigh almost nothing here. Small and vulnerable in the face of the hugeness of this strange environment, yet I'm empowered too.

Watching through my face mask, I enter into another world. The sunlight which warms my back dapples right to the sandy sea floor, spotlighting here the stillness of a camouflaged flat-fish, there a crab darting sideways, predatory yet so comical. I drift above cliffs where dark weed first hides, then reveals anemones. Swift fishes dart out to beguile with their shining beauty, or startle with their knobbly ugliness.

I swim up channels where the water temperature changes from warm to cool and back again. At one moment the weed brushes my stomach and the next a hundred feet of deepening blue water opens up below me. Tiny, almost transparent fish swim all around; some nibble gently at my toes. They wheel in silver schools, while the neons flash rainbow colours. This little one shows me its heart beating through a body almost as transparent as the water itself.

I come from another world above the surface, where we aliens breathe air and different rules govern almost everything. Here there's so much to explore. As yet I've dared go only a little way from shore. I know that, beyond this continental shelf, strange creatures exist in troughs which never see the sunlight.

Channelling between Africa and Europe, this sea merges eventually with both tropical lagoons and the plankton-filled deeps below ice fields, where penguins dive and fly. The species which make this earth's oceans their home, who could count them? Who could measure the volume of water, or number the grains of sand? All seven seas hold secrets, currents, caverns, storms, so I have surrendered my body to an untameable immensity.

I pray that you may have the power to comprehend, with all the saints, what is the breadth and length and height and depth, and to know the love of Christ that surpasses knowledge, so that you may be filled with all the fullness of God.

Ephesians 3:18–19

Meditation

From early times, right through to our hymns and songs of today, Christians have likened God's love to an ocean. Yet that imagery appears nowhere in the Bible, perhaps because the Jewish people feared the sea and believed it to be full of monsters—not the right message at all!

To Isaac of Syria, writing in the seventh century, the ocean spoke of God's love:

As a handful of sand thrown into the ocean, so are the sins of all flesh as compared with the mind of God.

Just as a strongly flowing fountain is not blocked up by a handful of earth, so the compassion of the Creator is not overcome by the wickedness of his creatures.

Isaac of Syria (7th century)

In the verses from Ephesians, quoted above, Paul expresses a prayer of breathtaking audacity. Obviously he had faith that *we* could be filled with the breadth and length and height and depth of the love of Christ, the Christ who fills all in all, the Christ whose love can't be contained by any ocean... any galaxy! If his ocean of love is pouring into our lives, it will stretch us beyond anything we could imagine. Even thinking about it takes us into another dimension, beyond time and space, into eternity! And eternity starts now!

Charles Finney (1792–1875) wrote in his *Memoirs* about an experience of the love of Christ which transformed him. He was alone in his law office after his conversion in 1821, when suddenly:

> *I could feel the impression, like a wave of electricity, going through and through me. Indeed, it seemed to come in waves and waves of liquid love; for I could not express it in any other way. It seemed like the very breath of God. I can recollect distinctly that it seemed to fan me, like immense wings.*
>
> *No words can express the wonderful love that was shed abroad in my heart. I wept aloud with joy and with love; and I do not know but I should say, I literally bellowed out the unutterable gushings of my heart. The waves came over me, and over me, one after the other, until I recollect I cried out, 'I shall die if these waves continue to pass over me.'*

Finney didn't die, not then. He spent his life leading thousands to Christ, right across America.

Exultation is the going
Of an inland soul to sea,
Past the houses—past the headlands—
Into deep Eternity—
Bred as we, among the mountains,
Can the sailor understand
The divine intoxication
Of the first league out from land?

'Exultation', by Emily Dickinson
(1830–86)

A GOD OF BLESSINGS

A Blessing from the Old Testament

The Lord bless you and keep you;
the Lord make his face to shine upon you,
and be gracious to you;
the Lord lift up his countenance upon you,
and give you peace.

Numbers 6:24–26

A Blessing from the New Testament

The grace of the Lord Jesus Christ, the love of God,
and the communion of the Holy Spirit be with all of you.

2 Corinthians 13:13

Meditation

Having meditated on different aspects of the love of God while writing this book, I'm convinced that he is a God who longs to bless and not to curse. He longs to gift us with his love. We block that love, that blessing, by standing with our arms folded or our head hung, perhaps because we feel unworthy, or hurt, or bitter, or indifferent. If only we would stand with arms open and face smiling in welcome, like children eager to receive Christmas presents!

However, the presents he gives are seldom what we expect. Since he often gives us part of himself, his blessings may seem worse at first, but then prove far better than we could ever imagine.

> *A cliché in red and gold packaging,*
> *Illusion of rich cosiness, unpeeled*
> *Reveals the object*
> *Of a desire, designed to satisfy—*
> *For ten minutes.*
>
> *Unmarketable the true gift,*
> *A tattered flower. It hides a dust of seeds.*
> *A baby crying, a young man dying.*
> *From this strange present,*
> *Who grows eternity?*

'Christmas Present', by Christine Leonard

I wrote that poem one autumn, ready to go in my Christmas cards. Then, at the end of November, the healthy fourteen-year-old son of some friends died suddenly in his sleep. A blood vessel had burst in his brain. Matthew, a fine Christian lad, was only months older than my own son. As I grieved and asked, 'why?' I saw a new poignancy in the poem.

God's love, his blessing, isn't something that comes cheaply. Yes, it's a free gift—but still it costs the recipient dearly, just as the free gift of a baby costs the parents more than they ever imagine. There's no way round it, because love is like that. Love cost God everything, from the end of his peaceful existence to the agonizing death of his Son. If we embrace his love we share not only in his joy but in the cost as well. His cup of blessing is heady wine on the one hand and the symbol of something too awful to contemplate on the other. As we drink that cup willingly, letting his love change us, we too may be broken. When we begin to feel only a little of the love he feels for others, we too will bleed and our hearts will break.

> *The cup of blessing that we bless, is it not a sharing in the blood of Christ? The bread that we break, is it not a sharing in the body of Christ?*

1 Corinthians 10:16

His love, his blessing, doesn't open the door to a trouble-free existence. If life is 'the vale of soul-making', being pampered on a kind of endless Caribbean cruise wouldn't do us much good in the end. Maybe that's why sometimes his blessings come in strange disguises, turning our lives and our thinking upside down.

After all, Jesus said:

> *'Blessed are the poor in spirit, for theirs is the kingdom of heaven.*
> *'Blessed are those who mourn, for they will be comforted.*
> *'Blessed are the meek, for they will inherit the earth.*
> *'Blessed are those who hunger and thirst for righteousness,*
> *for they will be filled.*
> *'Blessed are the merciful, for they will receive mercy.*
> *'Blessed are the pure in heart, for they will see God.*
> *'Blessed are the peacemakers, for they will be called children of God.*
> *'Blessed are those who are persecuted for righteousness' sake, for theirs*
> *is the kingdom of heaven.*
> *'Blessed are you when people revile you and persecute you and utter all*
> *kinds of evil against you falsely on my account. Rejoice and be glad, for*
> *your reward is great in heaven...'*

Matthew 5:3–11

What is he saying? That he blesses us especially when our circumstances appear to be anything but happy? One thing is sure, while his love and blessing sometimes come in ways we wouldn't expect or ask for, they are never gifts to be kept locked away for ourselves. In fact they multiply when we start giving them away to others. It's

often this new-found ability to come alongside others which starts
to make sense of some of our questions about times when we ourselves have suffered:

*Blessed be the God and Father of our Lord Jesus Christ, the Father of
mercies and God of all comfort, who comforts us in all our tribulation,
that we may be able to comfort those who are in any trouble, with the
comfort with which we ourselves are comforted by God. For as the
sufferings of Christ abound in us, so our consolation also abounds
through Christ.*

2 Corinthians 1:3–5 (NKJ)

Christ's strength ('comfort') is there for us no matter what happens—and not just for ourselves. He knows what we are going
through and his love, given to us, is always to be shared with
others. Like the loaves and fishes, his blessing multiplies when it
is given out and passed on. Being affirmed in God's love, basking
in it may sound selfish, but it's the foundation of his kingdom, for
how can you pass something on unless you have received it first?

Love be in my head, and in my understanding.
Love be in mine eyes and in my looking.
Love be in my mouth and in my speaking.
Love be in my heart and in my thinking.
Love be at mine end and at my departing.

Traditional

Another way his blessings multiply is through our thankfulness—
and not just when we grit our teeth and thank him very nicely
for those 'blessings in disguise'! All of us have some good, happy,
secure, beautiful, wonderful things in our lives. I, for one, can so
easily take these for granted and spend my energy worrying about
what might go wrong! It's often by appreciating our blessings that
we grow in faith and so find ourselves better able to help others.

Father, thank you for all the ways in which you have blessed my life. As I take a few moments to think about these, help me to bring them to mind. I name some of them now...

Thank you for all the ways in which you will continue to bless me in the future. I can only respond by wanting to bless, not only others, but you, Lord! That's not such a crazy thought—your word says that your people can bless you! May the driving force of my life, the prime motivation in all that I do be love and thankfulness towards Jesus, who said:

You shall love the Lord your God with all your heart, and with all your soul, and with all your mind, and with all your strength... and you shall love your neighbour as yourself.

Mark 12:30, 31

Bless the Lord, O my soul,
and all that is within me,
bless his holy name.
Bless the Lord, O my soul,
and do not forget all his benefits—
who forgives all your iniquity,
who heals all your diseases,
who redeems your life from the Pit,
who crowns you with steadfast love and mercy,
who satisfies you with good as long as you live
so that your youth is renewed like the eagle's.

Psalm 103:1–5

EPILOGUE

O Lord, Seek Us

O Lord, seek us, O Lord, find us
In thy patient care;
Be thy love before, behind us,
Round us everywhere:
Lest the god of this world blind us
Lest he speak us fair,
Lest he forge a chain to bind us,
Lest he bait a snare.
Turn not from us, call to mind us,
Find, embrace us, bear;
Be thy love before, behind us,
Round us, everywhere.

Christina Rossetti (1830–94)

Acknowledgments

We would like to thank all those who have given us permission to include quotations in this book. Every effort has been made to trace and acknowledge copyright holders. We apologize for any errors or omissions that may remain, and would ask those concerned to contact the publishers, who will ensure that full acknowledgment is made in the future.

Unless otherwise stated, scripture quotations are taken from the *New Revised Standard Version* of the Bible, copyright © 1989 by the Division of Christian Education of the National Council of the Churches of Christ in the USA. Used by permission.

Scripture text marked (RSV) is from *The Revised Standard Version* of the Bible, copyright © 1946, 1952, 1971 by the Division of Christian Education of the National Council of the Churches of Christ in the USA. Used by permission.

Scripture text marked (CEV) is from The Contemporary English Version, copyright © American Bible Society 1991, 1992, 1995. Anglicization copyright © British and Foreign Bible Society 1996. Used by permission.

Scripture text marked (NKJ) is from the New King James Version, copyright © 1979, 1980, 1982 by Thomas Nelson, Inc. Used by permission. All rights reserved.

Jesus of the Deep Forest: Prayer and Praises of Afua Kuma, trs. Fr Jon Kirby SVD. Published by Asempa Publishers, Box 919, Accra, Ghana. Extract used by permission. 'Children' © Roma Bell. Used by permission. 'And God said No' © Olive Dean. 'I "see" God's loving face...' and 'In a night of pain...' © L.D. Used by permission. Extract from 'I Cannot Tell' by William Young Fullerton. 'The Voice on the Mountain' © Eric Leat. Used by permission. 'The Love of God' and 'God's Love' © Janine Madge. Used by permission. 'Forgive us if we say...' from *When You Walk* by Adrian Plass, published by BRF. Copyright © Adrian Plass. Used by permission. 'We need to spend some time together...' © Tricia Richards. Used by permission. 'Love' and 'Surprise Gift' by Marjorie Noel Williams. Used by permission of her two surviving children.

Index of poetry

First lines

Index of poetry and quotations

Titles

Index of authors

Index of main scripture quotations